Why I Am a Buddhist

Why I Am a Buddhist

No-Nonsense Buddhism
for Modern Living

Stephen T. Asma

WATKINS PUBLISHING
LONDON

This edition published in the UK 2011 by
Watkins Publishing, Sixth Floor, Castle House,
75–76 Wells Street, London W1T 3QH

First published by Hampton Roads Publishing Company, Inc.
Charlottesville, VA 22902, USA in 2010

1 3 5 7 9 10 8 6 4 2

Text design by Jerry Goldie

Printed and bound by Imago in China

British Library Cataloguing-in-Publication Data Available

ISBN: 978-1-907486-57-9

www.watkinspublishing.co.uk

Contents

For my Wen Rong Jin –
incomparable
and always inspiring.

Acknowledgments

As with all my books, I owe a debt of gratitude to my supportive family. Thanks to my parents Ed and Carol, my brothers Dave and Dan, and the extended Asma clan.

This book was written as a challenge from my editor Greg Brandenburgh, and I want to thank him for giving me an opportunity to better formulate my ideas. Caroline Pincus helped me improve the organization of the book. The remaining flaws are entirely my own.

I am grateful to Steve Kapelke, provost at Columbia College; my chair Lisa Brock; and Deans Cheryl Johnson-Odim and Deborah Holdstein. And a tip of the hat to other friends at Columbia College, including Sara Livingston, Garnet Kilberg Cohen, Kate Hamerton, Teresa Prados-Torreira, Micki Leventhal, Oscar Valdez, Krista Macewko, and Baheej Khleif. Special thanks goes to my excellent reading-group partners Tom Greif and Rami Gabriel. Our many readings and discussions indirectly helped to shape this book. And the friendship is invaluable.

Others need to be thanked: Alex Kafka, Kendrick Frazier, Raja Halwani, Gianofer Fields, Pei Lun, Michael Shermer, Donna Seaman, Jim Graham, Jim Krantz, Harold Henderson, *Doctor Swing*, and the inestimable *Academy of Fists*.

Finally, I acknowledge my greatest devotion, my son Julien. Tom Wolf once described a son who "made the terrible discovery that men make about their fathers sooner or later ... that the man before him was not an aging father but a boy, a boy much like himself, a boy who grew up and had a child of his own and, as best he could, out of a sense of duty and, perhaps love, adopted a role called Being a Father so that his child would have something mythical and infinitely important: a Protector, who would keep a lid on all the chaotic and catastrophic possibilities of life." My son won't discover all this for many years yet, but I hope, by then, the myth will have done its beautiful work.

Introduction

Why *I am a Buddhist*. If I saw this book on the shelf, I might be tempted to reply, "Who *cares?* I've never even heard of you." Maybe if I were Richard Gere, or Tina Turner, or Adam Yauch of the Beastie Boys, people would muster more curiosity. But even then, readers probably want to know why they themselves should be Buddhists, or at least why they should be impressed with Buddhism. Why should anybody be impressed with Buddhism? Why should we care? How can we benefit from the teachings of a sixth-century Indian philosopher? These are the implicit questions contained in the title of this book. These are the questions I aim to answer.

The title of this book is a positive play on the famous polemical work by Bertrand Russell, *Why I am Not a Christian*. Positive or negative, praise or critique, such books are attempts to sketch the essence or core ideas of a worldview. Brush strokes are necessarily broad, but hopefully accurate. Exceptions to my generalizations will be inevitable, and the absence of someone's favorite Buddhist story, thinker, or text will be maddening to the initiated. But no matter the flaws of such a format, such a book will hopefully do two things well: first, introduce unfamiliar ideas to the novice, and second, remind and inspire the old hand.

The third possible function of such a personal book is to show how someone applies, or puts into practice, the theoretical teachings. Everyone knows that talking the talk is not the same as walking the walk, and, of course, each person will perambulate a little differently. But one value of such a book is to offer a model (albeit highly flawed) for how to translate the abstractions of Buddhism into concrete, usable life strategies.

Frankly, I probably seem like an odd Buddhist. Whenever I mention it in conversation, people respond with incredulity. Apparently, I should look more diminutive, speak in more hushed tones, and garland myself more with hippy swag. Many Westerners who have adopted Buddhism are remarkably humorless brown-rice eaters, who look like they wake up every morning and say "no" to life. In short, they are masochistic personalities. But this should not be taken, by the rest of us, as a strike against Buddhism. These characters would practice any religion in the same cheerless manner. I'm not one of these severe Buddhists. I'm not a monk, or even a member of a temple. I have studied Buddhism with some amazing scholars and practitioners, and I've taught Buddhism for many years in the States and Asia – but I think gurus are screwballs. I probably drink too much, and I'm not in the least bit interested in sexual abstinence. I like the White Sox, and I eat meat. If a guy like me can be a Buddhist … trust me, there's room for you.

A Chicago Buddhism

In a previous book, I mentioned that one of my goals was to "take the California out of Buddhism." Naturally, this got me in some hot water with Californians, and it appears to have endeared me to other grouchy cynics. But make no mistake, I like California and Californians. Unfortunately, the stereotype of their guileless, sunny affirmation of absolutely everything has become linked with Eastern spirituality. Beatniks and hippies have always been charmed by Buddhism. But Hollywood celebrities and San Francisco bohos have added a whole new dimension of credulity.

I've tried to offer a corrective counterbalance to all the hippy associations by suggesting a kind of blue-collar "Chicago Buddhism." Poet Carl Sandburg famously referred to Chicago as the "city of big shoulders." He called it "stormy, husky, brawling" – not to mention "crooked," "brutal," and "wicked." Despite all that, he sneered at Chicago's critics and said, "Come and show me another city with lifted head singing so proud to be alive and coarse and strong and cunning."

Of course, calling for a more Chicago-style Buddhism does not have much to do with actual geographical place, but more to do with frame of mind and disposition. I simply want to assure readers that one does not need to acquire hippy values in order to become a Buddhist. And, of course, this is also a wake-up call to the granola-types who think their prayer beads and Ravi Shankar records automatically qualify them for good standing with the dharma.

Buddhism as a Second Language, Buddhism as a First Language

Like many Western Buddhists, I first came to understand the fundamentals of the *dharma* by reading books. Most Western Buddhists have grown up in families that were monotheistic, culturally speaking, and we discovered our Buddhism via the printed word rather than at the neighborhood temple or wat or shrine. Religions are like languages – everyone has a first language, learned without much conscious effort and drawn upon like oxygen. But, if we're lucky we can adopt a second language, studying the grammar explicitly and memorizing the vocabulary until we feel comfortable in an entirely new atmosphere. Part of the attraction of Buddhism, for Westerners, has been its exotic character. Switching from Christianity to Islam, or vice versa, is dramatic, but not like adopting Buddhism. The basic metaphysical commitments of Islam, Christianity, and Judaism are surprisingly similar, even if their differences on the messiah/prophet issue have engendered a history of bloodletting. But the metaphysical ideas in Buddhism are nothing like Western monotheism, and the whole system of Eastern beliefs has an undeniably bohemian attraction. For my generation, part of the allure of Buddhism was that it mystified and irritated our parents. Thankfully, there are better reasons for being Buddhist than simply annoying one's parents, or this would be a very short book. But it will be funny to watch as our own children yawn about our second-language Buddhism, and perhaps rebel by diving headlong into the monotheism of their grandparents' generation.

Book learning, however, was only my *first* phase of Buddhology, and I have been fortunate enough to subsequently study the *dharma* traditions in Thailand, Laos, Cambodia, Vietnam, and China. In these countries, Buddhism is the people's "first language." Like my own Christianity, they have imbibed their Buddhism with their mother's milk and they possess an almost unconscious cultural familiarity with it. Buddhism is not exotic to them. It has no bohemian attraction. And they do not learn their Buddhism from books, but usually just absorb it by osmosis. They are cultural Buddhists.

Buddhism looks very different in these two populations – the native and the adoptive. Westerners tend to stress the psychological aspects of Buddhism, and lay great emphasis upon meditation. In contrast, native Buddhists in the lay population (i.e., the majority of Buddhists) are rarely found meditating or musing upon psychology, and instead tend to stress the devotional and ritualistic aspects of their religion.

Throughout this book I will try to acknowledge some of the more interesting deviations between "first-language" (cultural) Buddhism and "second-language" Buddhism. Tracking some of these differences helps us decode a lot of confusing and contradictory impressions that crowd together under the umbrella of "Buddhism." How is it, for example, that pacifist monks like the Dalai Lama, but also ass-kicking Kung Fu masters, and Japanese calligraphers, and mantra-chanting mystics, and hard-nosed atheists, and ascetic vegetarians, and unapologetic meat-eaters can all live under the flag of Buddhism? I will try to untangle some of this elaborate knot, wherever it seems productive to do so. But generally speaking, my goal is to discuss the philosophical core ideas put forth by Siddhartha Gautama Buddha (563–483 BCE).

The Dharma in Our Consumer Culture

Buddhism has a core set of elements that inform its approach to life, and these were not just recommended on the authority of the Buddha's charismatic personality. They were put forth, using argument and evidence, as testable and verifiable truths that could be corroborated by anyone who cared to investigate them. In that sense, Buddhism is not a set of beliefs to be adopted by faith, but a set of practices and beliefs to be tested and then employed in our pursuit of the good life.

I will slowly unpack these elements of Buddhism (collectively referred to as the *dharma*) by looking at some specific challenges of our modern life. How can Buddhism be applied to our lives in the workplace? How can Buddhism inform and ameliorate our increasing biotech moral quandaries (genetic therapy, stem cell research, mood medications, nanotechnology, etc.)? How can Buddhism help Americans in the "war of the sexes" and the ongoing reformulation of the family? How can Buddhism, with its emphasis on conflict resolution, contribute to and clarify such issues as "nation-building," "religious tolerance," and the "war on terror"? And how can Buddhism better educate or moderate our national pastimes of entertainment and consumption? Buddhism has beneficial wisdom to help us navigate even the most arduous aspects of modern life.

While I was writing this book, a news story filled the media – the same story that fills the media every year around Thanksgiving. The day after the holiday is celebrated as the high holy-day of consumerism – Black Friday. Consumers line up all night long outside retail stores, and when the stores open, the patrons, filled to the brim with cravings, actually trample each other in a stampede to get the consumer products. This time around an employee at a superstore was actually crushed to death. When patrons of the superstore were informed of the tragedy, they disregarded the management's attempt to close the store and instead went on shopping – refusing to leave. Many lesser injuries ensued all around the country. While everyone in the media and the wider culture dutifully reported the death and the injuries with gravitas, there was no question or critique of the larger ideological assumption – furious consumption is healthy for America. If anyone doubts the relevance of Buddhism for Americans, I recommend they spend some time watching the depressing YouTube videos of people getting trampled in order to get TVs and video games.

Beginning to Hear the Real Music

I want to promote the idea that Buddhism, while born on the other side of the planet, is truly relevant and available to us. But real Buddhism is not for the dabbler – that is to say, it cannot be tried on for a week and then discarded. I'm not recommending that we all sell our stuff and head for the jungles of Thailand in order to demonstrate our seriousness about Buddhism. But Buddhism is not a "turn on, tune in, and drop out" philosophy that we can attain effortlessly. Learning to apply Buddhism is like learning to play an instrument. It takes a while to get the fundamentals – scales, chords, and fingering technique. Then it takes daily practice to learn melodies and progressions. Prolonged failure and frustration are inevitable, but very slowly one begins to hear real music. We don't have to become virtuosos on our instruments or Buddhist sages to appreciate and employ the artform in our lives, but we can't achieve anything without effort.

The Buddha offers a simile (*Sedaka Sutta,* SN 47.20) to demonstrate how difficult, demanding, and almost unnatural it is to achieve the state of mindfulness in daily life. Imagine, he says, that you have come to the town square and discover a big crowd of people gathered around a stage performance. The crowd is clamoring that the most beautiful celebrity has just arrived, and now she is performing a provocative dance. You are naturally drawn to witness the exciting show, but before you can glimpse anything you are pulled aside. You are informed that you must carry a bowl on your head filled to the brim with oil, and you must carry it on the narrow path between the beautiful celebrity and the writhing crowd. A man with a raised sword will follow directly behind you, and if you spill a drop he will cut off your head.

After relating this weird story, the Buddha asks us if we would let ourselves be distracted from the precarious oil bowl. Obviously, our necks are on the line, so there is much at stake. But it is this kind of intense focus and dedication that mindful meditation (*sati*) requires of us. The sword-wielding threat is an artificial and metaphorical way of representing the drastic reorientation of our values and our actions – away from desire and idle curiosity and toward awareness and attention to the present moment.

The trained mind can rise above distraction and craving, but the normal mind is fraught with temptations, agitations, and diversions. The idea of not looking at a beautiful woman (or man) when we are clearly drawn in that direction may sound rather puritanical. But the point of the simile is not to denigrate beauty, but to isolate the tension between natural inclination and discipline. It is perfectly natural to look at beautiful people, and Buddhism doesn't require the forfeit of such trouble-free pleasures. I suspect that our very biology ensures that we'll take a quick gander at any attractive prospect, and such radar abilities probably had some evolutionary advantages for our ancestors. But if I simply *cannot help myself* from gawking at a stunning model on the street, then I have overturned a division of labor inside myself. I have become the servant of my desire, rather than being the master of my desire. I am being led, rather than leading.

Of course, this example of the wandering eye is rather frivolous. Every husband I know has mastered the art of blinder-vision when his vigilant wife and he pass by beautiful women on the street. If he hasn't trained himself yet, his wife will be happy to act as the head-chopping tutor. But even in this frivolous case, we can see the seeds of the more serious psychological tension between desire and discipline.

Buddhism attempts to give us a second nature – one that writes over the old genetic and psychological code. It never asks us to pretend that the old code doesn't exist. Unlike some other religions, it doesn't imagine humans in some unrealistic angelic form. Nor does it cast us as weak and fallen souls, incapable of any improvement save those delivered by an almighty deity. Buddhism acknowledges that we are filled with some pernicious stuff, but we can discipline our minds in a way that liberates us from our tendency to cause suffering. The benefits of this approach can be seen in our emotional, social, spiritual lives. One of the main reasons why we fail to attain our goals, for example, is because our own appetites pull us off our chosen path. Actualizing our potential is a large part of happiness, and Buddhism helps us chart realistic goals and also gives us tools for staying on course.

Achieving this second nature of mindfulness may

ultimately be as urgent as keeping the bowl of oil steady, but mercifully we all get to try again if we screw it up. With regard to beautiful women and many other temptations, I have spilled the oil countless times. But I've also occasionally found some power and freedom in the ability to "check myself before I wreck myself."

This book is not going to stand behind you with sword at the ready. I haven't done that to myself, so I'm certainly not going to get preachy with you. I'm a fan of the gentle but persistent application of dharma – the Middle Way between the zealot and slacker approaches.

Chapter 1

A Newly Elevated Status for My Private Little Soul

Discovering Transcendentalism

To escape the alienation of high school, I enrolled in one of the available subcultures. Subcultures were, and are, great consolations to teenage angst. Some of my friends chose Goth subculture as a palliative – dyed black hair, black lipstick, black garments, clothes-pins pierced in ears and cheeks, and a whole genre of music that celebrated the Romantic version of the misunderstood individual. While some of the Goth aesthetic and ideology appealed to me, the idea of dressing up in a costume at the age of sixteen struck me as too desperate. I was also just too lazy to spend time making myself look like a corpse.

The other big subcultures in the 1980s included the neo-hippies, the New Wave, the heavy metal kids, and the lingering punk culture. I chose the consolations of hippy life, spending a couple summers tripping on mushrooms, camping out, and watching Jerry Garcia noodle his way into occasionally sublime musical territories. I was attracted to the improvisational aspect of the music and, of course, the dropout aspect of the unshowered fan culture (although I didn't see why we couldn't say no to the oppressive shackles of society *and* still attend to the personal hygiene thing).

Most alienated kids are looking for some subculture that announces to their parents, and every other authority figure, that "you're not the boss of me!" Heavy metal culture did so, like punk, with defiant fists raised. There's nothing like a good aggressive punch-up at some booze-soaked party to establish your rebel credibility. But hippy defiance is more gentle – it's the wispy, dervish dance of the deadhead who is way too stoned to punch anybody.

Neo-hippy culture introduced me to the ideas and writings of proto-hippies like Henry David Thoreau, but also the more proximate countercultural icons like Timothy Leary, Ram Dass, Allen Ginsberg, and other proponents of mystical awareness. One of the great things about many high school subcultures is that they tend toward intellectualism. Goths tended to read books, as did metal fans, punks, and hippy stoners. These days, I'm sure the Internet provides even greater opportunities for alienated youth to reach beyond their stultifying local cliques and find kindred spirits of every freethinking variety.

The Buddha himself can be seen as a young man who also grew weary of his own tiny world, and who longed to break free to the wider realms of possibility. Born in 563 BCE in Kapilavastu to a wealthy family, Prince Gautama was sheltered and kept in virtual isolation throughout his early life. While his isolation was filled with the luxuries and pleasures that privilege affords, he was nonetheless channeled into a predetermined path of education, marriage, fatherhood, and business ambition. He had a bourgeois life in store for him, but it was not to be.

Despite his overprotective father's plans, Gautama made a chariot expedition outside the palace walls and there encountered three deeply powerful sights. First, he saw a very old man, struggling and laboring with infirmed limbs, hunched back, and downturned head. The young prince was shocked by this experience. When the chariot driver explained to him that all people eventually end up in this decaying condition, he grew despondent. Next he happened to catch sight of a maimed person, and again he was surprised and depressed. Lastly, Gautama came across a rotting corpse lying in the street. He was shocked to realize that he and everyone he knew and loved would one day be just like this decomposing carcass. It was these three experiences – age, injury, and death – that wrenched Gautama out of his sheltered existence and forced him to renounce luxury and leave the palace to find a cure for suffering. Obviously teen angst is only one, rather trifling, form of suffering, and the Buddha had much bigger fish to fry. But the antinomian urge to emancipate oneself and get to some more essential truth is quite common in disaffected teenagers. The Buddha's quest is always appealing in that sense.

Before I could reach real Buddhism, however, I had to wade through a wonderful swamp of mystical experiences and transcendental philosophies. This chapter is a brief tour of my youthful evolution from an other-worldly adolescent theologian to a down-to-earth spiritualist. It's important to sketch this journey because so many other people will recognize themselves in this same meandering odyssey. But more important, as we'll see, the Buddha himself made the same basic sequence of steps. He was first attracted to transcendental theologies of God and soul, then he gradually became disenchanted, and finally he rejected them in favor of a new this-worldly enchantment. Part of why I am a Buddhist is that I unwittingly went on this same kind of journey.

Knocking on the Doors of Perception

Like many people I spent my teen years greedily knocking on all the inner doors of perception. A steady diet of George

Harrison's spooky sitar tunes, drug experimentation, and surrealist art eventually led me to have a series of mystical experiences when I was sixteen and seventeen years old. Once, during a Peter Gabriel concert in the early 1980s, I seemed to experience the melting away of the subject/object distinction – the thousands of fans, bathed in an eerie blue light while undulating to some tribal rhythm, all melted together into a giant living organism. Many will attest to the fact that collective dance and music really seem to dissolve the ego in a pleasing way.

I also tried floating in a sensory deprivation tank. These tanks are filled with a thick saline solution that makes a person float suspended in the water, and they are kept at the same temperature as the human body. The inside is closed off to any outside light or sound. You crawl into the tank naked and slowly lie down flat in the salt water so that the body is entirely submerged, but the face is exposed in order to breathe. Since you are suspended in a fluid that is the same temperature as your body, you eventually lose track of where your body begins and ends. There is no point of contact with any stimulus – no shirt to rub on your neck, no chair to press on your butt, no pants to ride up on you, no glasses to pressure your face, and so on. Your tactile senses slowly fade away. So, too, your sense of sight slips away, because it's pitchblack inside. And your sense of hearing recedes because your ears are plugged and underwater.

The first time I tried this weird experiment, I lay down too quickly, accidentally got burning saltwater in my eyes, thrashed around like a hooked pike, and accidentally kicked off the roof of the fiberglass tank. Many subsequent trips to the deprivation tank, however, led to some interesting alterations of consciousness. I discovered firsthand, for example, that my thoughts could race at frightening speeds and along bizarre chains of association if they were not momentarily distracted and redirected by external sensory stimuli. In any ordinary experience, we are constantly tapped, poked, and nudged by tactile stimuli, or sounds, or sights, or smells. And these sensations are always quietly deviating and swerving our internal thought dialogue. But if you remove them altogether, then thoughts race in unfamiliar ways.

After about six or seven sessions in the sensory deprivation tank, I had a truly unique experience. I took it to be rather mystical in nature, but even then, during my most credulous era, I couldn't be sure about it. It was basically comprised of three qualitatively different "moments." First, my mind was spiraling in its usual out-of-control race of thoughts. Then utter black *nothingness*. Then a jerky and staggered return of the spiraling race of thoughts – which now included "what the hell was that?" The duration of these moments was impossible to tell. When you have no sensory inputs, you cannot measure time at all. A minute can feel like an hour, and an hour can feel like a minute – time becomes largely subjective and obscure. It felt to me like I was gone for a good long time, but I have no way of knowing.

Did I merge momentarily with God? Did I melt into the great emptiness of all things? Did I now know, as the Beatles had sung in "She Said She Said," what it's like to be dead? Or had I, more likely, just fallen asleep and then woken up again? The problem with experiencing the great unconditioned reality that lies beyond our ordinary doors of perception is that it has no features or qualities or souvenirs that you can bring back with you. So it may be that you haven't really gone anywhere.

At the time, however, I was marginally convinced that I had had some kind of experiential corroboration of a spiritual reality. I felt that some momentary encounter with the divine had been achieved, even if the content of that encounter was empty – or was it perfectly *full?*

I was ripe for such communion because I had been raised as a devout Catholic. Some people think that the conventional and conservative experience of Catholicism and the eccentric, lefty spiritualism of hippy culture are worlds apart. But, in fact, Catholics have a deep sense of mystery in the very belly of their religion. Unlike most Protestants, Catholics give themselves over to the irrational mystery, miracle, and authority. There is an undeniably conventional and institutional aspect of Catholicism, but beneath its traditionalism is a robust mystical approach to God.

When I was in primary and middle school I was an altar boy and even a lector. When I began to ask philosophical questions in my early teens, my blue-collar parents knew of no other outlet for such precocious intellectualism except perhaps the priesthood. I was dutifully driven to the local seminary to meet with priests and be interviewed to see if I had the calling. I didn't.

I had a variety of awkward conversations with priests, in which I asked them honest but difficult theological questions. Each cleric in turn was genuinely charitable with his time and his learning, but none of them could answer my pressing queries. For example, I wanted to know whether God *made up* the Ten Commandments or whether he *discovered* them. It seems like a trivial point, perhaps, but I had read enough to know that this was an old dilemma. If the all-powerful God freely makes up right and wrong, then, theoretically, he could change his mind and reverse the list. In principle, he could decide that coveting your neighbor's wife was now good and resting on the Sabbath was now bad. They're his rules after all, and he could (like my father) suddenly change the rules if he wanted to. This means that there is nothing intrinsically good or bad about the Ten Commandments, they are just the edicts of the most powerful king. Alternatively, if God *discovered* the rules, it preserves the idea that right and wrong are objective and intrinsic truths, but it also suggests that they are independent of God. On this version, God has done the research, discovered the good, and then reported back to us like a mere messenger.

After trying unsuccessfully to get off the horns of this dilemma, priests would invariably ask me to simply pray harder and ask for grace. These sorts of evasions are highly effective with polite adults, but youthful, impolite, determination always led me to sustain the interrogation. Because my grandmother was convinced that Jews, Hindus, Communists, and all pagans would eventually burn in Hell, I was always keen to press a man-of-the-cloth on this doctrinal point. My grandmother, it turns out, had a rather draconian sense of posthumous justice, but even the priests' more tempered version about Purgatory seemed to me to be highly unfair to the unwitting Bushmen, Chinese, Brahmins, and everybody born before Jesus. I had to agree with Charles Darwin's famous quip: "I can indeed hardly see how anyone ought to wish Christianity to be true; for if so the plain language of the text seems to show that the men who do not believe, and this would include my father, brother and almost all my best friends, will be everlastingly punished. And this is a damnable doctrine." The more I read about different cultures and religions, the more naive my own Catholicism seemed. Christian theology didn't seem wrong, so much as provincial.

But the sense of mystery remained strong in me, even after my doctrinal disappointments. Like many Americans, or other people living in pluralistic societies, I began to create a pastiche religion from the bits of theology floating around in the melting pot. So when my high school flirtation with hippy culture exposed me to the folksy bong-wisdom of nature worship, I merely connected it to my ideas about a transcendent God, and the soul, and all that. The result was that my mind was prepared to experience something "transcendent," but my allegiance to any one dogma had already fallen away – so I was not forced into a specific theological interpretation of mystical experiences. I consider this a happy accident in the timing of my philosophical development.

If I had fallen in with a group of high school stoners that got lit up in order to loiter in the parking lot of the local mall, I could have missed the taste of higher consciousness altogether. But as it so happens, I chanced to fall in with some aesthetes and we used psychedelics to enhance our nature hikes, our museum trips, and, most important, our own artistic endeavors. We grew our hair long and formed a band that played improvisational hippy jams late into the night until my long-suffering father would yell at us to shut up and get haircuts too.

What all this meant is that a wonderful association formed in me – one that many people have experienced. It is the association of *ecstasy* in music and the same kind of experience in the spiritual traditions. Many people have noticed that the mystical experience, or peak experience, or oceanic feeling can be accessed via several different pathways, including art, sex, religion, and, of course, intoxicants. Late-night jam sessions, spiked with psychotropics, led to meditations on the oneness of all things, the infinite grandeur of reality, and other trippy realizations.

Many sticks of incense later, I became disenchanted with neo-hippy culture. Perhaps the writing was on the wall from the very beginning, because anybody getting into hippy ideology in the 1980s quickly realized that the very best part of being a hippy, namely, *free love*, was no longer available to us. I came of age in the era of AIDS. Sex with strangers was liberating and enlightening in the late 1960s and 1970s, but my generation's sexual maturity was accompanied by the nagging worry that *fucking can kill you*. With the free love ingredient missing, hippy culture had paltry other virtues to offer.

I slowly gravitated to a tougher-minded form of musical improvisation – namely, jazz. And I simultaneously graduated to a tougher-minded mysticism, reading Aldous Huxley, Krishnamurti, and Thomas Merton. I wore out my copy of Somerset Maugham's *The Razor's Edge*. Once I had acquired a taste for that elusive transcendental experience, I pursued the well-worn path (trod earlier by the Maharishi-following Beatles) to Hinduism. I struggled with the *Vedas*, the *Upanishads*, and the *Bhagavad Gita*, the principal Hindu scriptures. Most Westerners think that the sacred scriptures of Hinduism are replete with mystical gems of wisdom about consciousness and reality. In truth, these passages comprise a small percentage of the overall amount, and an unguided dive into the Hindu scriptures turns up a staggering number of texts devoted to hygiene ablutions, fire-building rituals, horse care recommendations, and other mind-numbing daily life minutiae. Eventually, however, one finds the more philosophical passages and gets a sense of the metaphysics.

At first, Hinduism fit nicely with my romantic sensibility and it possessed features that reminded me of the best parts of monotheism. This world of experience, according to Hinduism, is a veil of illusion (*maya*). We might have wonderful pleasures and terrible losses in this material world, but we should understand that the material world itself is just an ephemeral bit of foam when compared with eternal reality. Hinduism claims that a highly disciplined mind can have communion with God. The *Bhagavad Gita* says, "When his mind is tranquil, perfect joy comes to the man of discipline; his passions are calmed, he is without sin, being one with the infinite spirit" (6th Teaching, #27).

Those ecstatic experiences that I found in music, drugs, and even sex could be, according to Hinduism, momentary connections to the divine. I fell for this stuff hard. Talk about a consoling subculture! The Goths and the heavy metal kids had nothing on this stuff. Losing the ego in ecstasy is the ultimate escape from alienation. Some people overcome their teen angst by getting a girlfriend – I sought to heal my estrangement from the whole universe. Obviously, I was a rather melodramatic lad. And I had finally discovered *transcendentalism*.

The Transcendental Temptation

Transcendentalism is a theory embraced by thinkers as diverse as Plato, St. Augustine, Ralph Waldo Emerson, and Vedantic Hindus. It posits the existence of two worlds instead of one. The physical world that we live in is, according to the transcendentalist, a corrupt copy of a more perfect world. My slowly decaying body, my material possessions, my faltering democracy, and my entire sensory experience, to take a range of examples, are all just fleeting shadows when compared to the ideal and perfect realm believed to exist by transcendentalists. This is not an obscure or uncommon theory. The vast majority of religious humans, both Eastern and Western, embrace some form of transcendentalism.

If you believe that God is in his heaven, that he created the physical universe and is in some sense above and beyond his creation, then you are a transcendental thinker.

In Hindu philosophy the transcendental being is called Brahman. Brahman is the permanent eternal reality that serves as the stable principle underlying the fluctuating world of material nature. The cosmos is always changing and becoming something new and different, but Brahman is the divine unity behind this veil of changing appearances. And in the same way that the cosmos has a persistent unchanging reality that is hidden from view, so, too, each human has a persistent unchanging reality hidden within. In the West we call the hidden reality within us the "soul" and in the East it is called *Atman*, or Self. My body may change its material composition from one year to the next (even from one day to the next), but a soul or *Atman* remains the same over the course of these changes and provides my source of personal identity (my self) over time. The *Gita* scripture explains that "our bodies are known to end, but the embodied self is enduring, indestructible, and immeasurable" and, "just as the embodied self enters childhood, youth, and old age, so does it enter another body; this does not confound a steadfast man" (2nd Teaching, #18 and 13). In other words, this inner core self is the real you, and it will go on to a new life in a new body after this one perishes.

Hindu philosophers (especially in the *Svetesvatara* and *Katha Upanishads*) recognized the common metaphysical functions of these permanent realities, Brahman and *Atman*. Ultimately, they concluded that God (Brahman) and Self (*Atman*) are one and the same substance or being. In other words, the permanent hidden soul/*Atman* inside me is actually a piece of God/Brahman itself. A bit of Brahman is living inside me as my divine soul and through moral perfection and wisdom I can release this soul (my true self) after death to rejoin its transcendent origin. The *Katha Upanishad* says, "The knowing self is never born; nor does he die at any time.He sprang from nothing and nothing sprang from him. He is unborn, eternal, abiding, and primeval. He is not slain when the body is slain." According to Hindu orthodoxy, my own moral weakness and persistent stupidity prevents the estranged bit of Brahman within me from reaching its home,and damns my soul to return again and again in subsequent lifetimes (reincarnation).

An influential Hindu scripture, the *Chandogya Upanishad,* puts the reincarnation issue bluntly. "And so those who behave nicely here will, in general, find a nice womb, the womb of a Brahmin or the womb of a prince (Kshatriya) or the womb of a merchant (Vaishya). But those whose behavior here is stinking will, in general, find a stinking womb, the womb of a dog or the womb of a pig or the womb of an Untouchable" (*Chandogya*, chapter 5).

If you are really righteous, however, you get out of this cycle (*samsara*) altogether. Hindu scriptures describe the eventual metaphysical reunion of Self and God (after countless lifetimes) to a drop of water returning to the ocean or a tiny spark returning to the eternal conflagration. And this final communion will be eternal bliss.

The belief in a soul, whether in its Eastern or Western version, is transcendentalist because it posits another reality beyond this mundane world of sensory experience. It suggests that my true self is some intangible undetectable being, having a similar metaphysical tint as God, which will eventually go to live in a world beyond.

How refreshing all this seemed when I was a teenager. It had the cool stuff from Catholicism – afterlife and eternal God – but also a newly elevated status for my own little private soul. The idea that my true self or soul really is God might seem overreaching from the point of view of Western theology, but it's awfully attractive and satisfying to the narcissist in every teenager.

Same as the Old Boss?

According to Hinduism, when we realize our true transcendental natures, we attain wisdom and better understand the false world of illusions that ordinarily pummel us. The values of the mundane world are superseded by the eternal transcendental values. This all sounds fine and good, and it's hard to think of any religion that doesn't subscribe to such a view, but to me there seemed to be a grave downside. To see the downside, consider one of the most famous episodes in Hindu poetry.

The *Bhagavad Gita* illustrates how this transcendental divine world, beyond the mortal coil, takes priority over, or *overrides*, this earthly world. The *Gita* tells the story of a military leader named Arjuna who finds himself leading an army against an opposing legion of his kinsmen. On the battlefield, just before combat, Arjuna confides to his chariot driver (the prophet Krishna in disguise) that he is morally conflicted about the impending battle. Why should he kill his cousins? Indeed, why should he kill at all? These deep apprehensions plague Arjuna's mind in the beginning of the text, and the remainder of the scripture is a series of arguments and revelations that Krishna offers to inspire Arjuna into battle. First, Krishna explains, Arjuna should kill his enemies because God says so – on the grounds of simple, straightforward, divine authority. Like Abraham in the Bible, who is instructed by God to sacrifice his son, Arjuna must demonstrate his devotion to the sacred, transcendental power.

The second explanation that Krishna offers involves the

realities of the Hindu caste, or class, system. Arjuna was born into the Kshatriya class, which means that it is his sacred *duty* to fulfill the actions of a warrior. In Hinduism, social caste is understood in cosmic terms, and the harmony of the universe itself is tied to the social harmony of each caste fulfilling its function or destiny. Without the execution of our sacred duties, the world itself slouches toward chaos.

Finally, Krishna attempts to assuage Arjuna's guilt over murdering his kinsmen by pointing out that it is only the physical body that gets destroyed. The soul, or *Atman*, of his kinsman is divine and eternal and will not perish by Arjuna's sword. In fact, the *Atman* will only be liberated by the killing of the body. The *Gita* explains, "This physical body is perishable. But the embodied soul is described as indestructible, eternal, and immeasurable. Therefore do fight. Neither the one who thinks it kills nor the one who thinks it is killed knows the truth. The soul neither kills nor gets killed. The soul is never born nor does it die at any time. It has neither past nor future. It is unborn, ever existing, permanent, and ancient … . Just as a man discards worn out clothes and puts on new clothes, the soul discards worn out bodies and wears new ones" (2nd Teaching).

Under this transcendental override, common sense, human compassion, peaceful diplomacy, and even the evidence of one's senses are all overridden by Arjuna's eventual acceptance of a transcendental God whose unfathomable commands require Arjuna to kill the enemy. The transcendental position here actually claims, in essence, that killing someone is doing that person *a favor* (because it releases the eternal self).

The harm that pious saints and theologians cause is staggering. Already, as a young man, I had seen the many ways that Catholic dogma led otherwise reasonable people to cause misery in their own families – all for the sake of upholding some abstract, remote piece of transcendental "truth." Everyone who grew up in a small parish has watched families get torn apart by holier-than-thou expectations of impossible moral righteousness. Fathers disown their daughters over abortions, grandmothers disown their grandchildren over divorces, hostility crushes filial intimacy when someone comes out as gay, and so on. The hypocrisy is not as troubling as the actual damage and suffering caused by so-called higher values.

So now, in my late teens, I was discovering the same sort of theologically based dehumanization in my adopted Hindu philosophy. I was raised on a Yahweh who told the devoted Abraham to kill his own son and who told Job to suck it up while Satan tortured him – now add to this a crucified savior who redeems everybody by bleeding out on a cross. And finally I had arrived at a Hindu God, Krishna, who was convincing a warrior that killing was actually an act of help-fulness. Meet the new boss, I thought to myself, same as the old boss. Why do the gods want so much blood?

Human suffering, in these transcendental traditions, always seemed to get whitewashed as either unreal or as worth it somehow, when the final communion with God occurs. When the lion lies down with the lamb, or when *Atman* rejoins Brahman, all this misery will be washed away, supposedly. Wasn't there any spiritually minded tradition that accepted the reality of human suffering, and then worked to decrease it?

An Ethical Meritocracy

Eventually, I discovered that Buddhism answered to this description. The Buddha waged a lifelong campaign against suffering, but not by inventing another transcendental world where suffering doesn't exist. We will look at his specific critiques of Hindu ideas like *Atman* and Brahman later in this book. But one of the first things I learned about the Buddha was that he opposed the caste system.

If he never did anything else, besides oppose the caste system, he still would have made it into my hero pantheon – which, at age seventeen, included mostly jazz musicians, mystics, comic book artists, and the occasional humanitarian.

The Buddha rejected the old Indian cosmology of permanent social classes. The Vedic tradition, which Gautama grew up in, embraced an anatomical metaphor for human society. Before our current world existed, according to legend, a gigantic primordial being named Purusha had lived for eons. Purusha was eventually sacrificed by the gods and carved up into pieces. His body became the Earth and the heavens and seas, but in particular his dismembered parts became the basis of the human social hierarchy. Purusha's head became the Brahmin (priestly) class, the warriors and the class of nobility (Kshatriyas) descended from the arms, the merchant and craft class (Vaishyas) from the thighs, and the laborers and untouchable classes from Purusha's ignoble dirty feet. It was imperative, according to Hindu thought, that individuals of each caste resign themselves to their respective stations in the cosmic order.

Gautama grew up in a world in which everyone was made to feel that some people were more valuable than others. Indian social life was not, and still is not, egalitarian. If you were born into an untouchable family, then you were destined to live with a certain stigma and you were expected to do a certain kind of labor – usually involving excrement removal, the handling of dead animals, and the like. If you were born into a Brahmin family, your life would be significantly easier. The doors of education, respect, and prosperity would be

open to you. Obviously the sense of righteousness and enti-
tlement in the upper classes must have been intolerably high.
After all, a Brahmin could imagine that his place of privilege
was written into the very fabric of the cosmos.

In response to cosmic smugness, the Buddha offered a radical new hierarchy – one that totally disrupted the old social cat-
egories. Some people may be better than others, he argued, but
their superiority is not based on caste. Instead, we should accord
greater respect on the basis of moral excellence. The Buddha
wanted a social revolution, wherein admiration and value
would be reassigned according to good actions rather than
genealogy. He did not call for a purely egalitarian society per
se, but for an equal opportunity society. He asked people to
examine more closely the actual social world, rather than the
entrenched ideological social picture. In doing so, he asked,
don't we find some Brahmins acting like complete scumbags
– selfish, liars, cheaters, and swindlers? And conversely, he asks,
haven't we met lowercaste folks who are profoundly good,
honest, charitable, compassionate, and so on? Ethical virtue cuts
across caste divisions and renders them irrelevant. This call for
a new kind of society was pretty attractive to everybody who
was *not* in the Brahmin caste, and this may account for some
of the early appeal of Buddhism. Outcasts who attained high
virtue, were regularly ordained in the early Buddhist community. Buddhism became an ethical meritocracy.

Against the Purusha cosmology of caste, Gautama offered an alternative version of our origins. In the *Agganna Sutta*, he tells an evolutionary story. Before the era of humans, as we know them, there was a species of luminous creatures – our indirect ancestors. These creatures, which were relatively similar to each other, lived in peaceful harmony. But they noticed a savory crust growing all over the Earth's surface, and the taste was delicious. As the luminous beings began to eat the crust, they began to grow more dense and heavy. With each meal, they acquired greater cravings for more and more of the food. Their bodies began to change radically and their mood became contentious and greedy. Eventually, they were attacking each other and competing in order to satisfy their growing desires. The greediest of the creatures found that their bodies had changed. Instead of similar luminous creatures, the new beings evolved into differentiated kinds – some beautiful and others ugly. Finally, the savory crust was all gone and new kinds of fungus grew on the planet and acted as food for the heavy, craving creatures. This new diet led to the evolution of sex, as we know it. Offspring no longer spontaneously emerged, as in the days of luminosity, but now pairs of creatures had to copulate with each other. *Desire* became the very substance of these new beings, the human beings.

This is a charming story, of course, but its purpose is,

among other things, to offer an alternative cosmology to describe our social and even biological differences. Excessive desire makes some of us less virtuous than others. Craving, not caste status, causes vice. And all of us have a large share of this craving, so nobody is born unblemished and genealogically pure. The Buddha is calling for some humility in the upper classes, and maybe a bit more pride in the lower classes.

The legend symbolizes the rejection of a cosmological justification of caste, but, of course, it's just a charming pre-scientific speculation. Taken literally, such origin stories, like our *Genesis* story, are just absurd. All such origin myths attempt, instead, to explain and justify certain values – individual, social, environmental.

The Buddha Ate Meat

One of the other values that Gautama wanted to increase (beyond the value of all humans) was the worth of all nonhuman life. In the *Kutadanta Sutta*, the Buddha encounters a Brahmin who is about to engage in a bloody traditional animal sacrifice, consisting of hundreds of bulls, hundreds of heifers, and hundreds of goats and rams. Gautama convinces the Brahmin that he should sacrifice and purify his own inner vices instead. No amount of animal blood will purify a man's heart of darkness. Work instead on the root causes, the Buddha teaches. The Brahmin is converted and sets his animals out to pasture, to eat the green grass and drink cool water. Not only were untouchables more valuable to the Buddha, but so were all living creatures. He took the *sacred* cloak off the Brahmins and threw it around the entire biosphere.

In the *Jataka Tales*, which are very allegorical scriptures – often used to educate children – the Buddha tells a cautionary story about sacrificing animals. One day a Brahmin began grooming a goat for sacrifice later that day at the Feast for the Dead. The goat began laughing during this grooming, and then suddenly started to cry. The Brahmin master was stunned and asked the goat to explain. "In times past," the goat explained, "I was a Brahmin, who taught the *Vedas* just like you. I, too, sacrificed a goat as an offering for a Feast of the Dead. Because of killing that single goat, I have had my head cut off four hundred and ninety-nine times. I laughed aloud when I realized that this is my last birth as an animal to be sacrificed. Today I will be freed from my misery." The goat goes on to say that his jocular outburst was suddenly crushed and he came to tears when he realized that the Brahmin master himself might now have to face five hundred future beheadings (*Matakabbhatta Jataka*, #18).

Respect for all life is a major plank in the foundation of Buddhism. Animal suffering is to be avoided at all costs. But the idea that Buddhists have always been, and always should be, *vegetarians* is pure myth. The historical Buddha, Siddhartha Gautama, ate meat – he even died eating meat. My Buddhist friends in Cambodia eat meat. Most Tibetan Buddhists eat meat. Meat, contrary to popular opinion, is not the problem for Buddhists. The problem is causing unneeded pain to animals, so if we can kill them humanely, then the ethical transgression is averted. In the West these days, you will meet many Buddhists who are smug lettuce-nibblers, and that's fine. But be assured, it is not Buddhism per se that compels their diet.

Enter Zen Buddhism: The Attraction of Being Here Now

When I first learned that the Buddha threw away the caste system in favor of a more observable ethical meritocracy, I felt the inevitable plucking on my American heartstrings. We Americans are all raised to champion egalitarian individualism. Plus, the overthrow of Brahmin authority meshed perfectly with my teenage rebellion and romantic dissent. Teen angst makes one identify with the outcasts in any story, so the Buddha's rebellion was an inspiration on that front as well. But, slowly, I began to notice something else in my attraction to Buddhism. The rejection of caste is a movement away from invisible transcendental systems and toward the actual world of lived experiences. Throwing out a metaphysical picture of humans (the cosmic caste system) in favor of the evidence of our senses (virtuous people come from every class) is a *scientific* move.

The Buddha used this empirical scientific approach to criticize the other transcendental beliefs of his day, namely, the beliefs in *Atman* and Brahman. But while I felt a growing attraction to this sixth-century rebel, I was not quite ready to give up the comforting ideas of permanent soul and permanent God. In my late teens, I wasn't intellectually sophisticated enough to take on too many metaphysical and epistemological questions. But as an artist, I began to gravitate more toward a specific form of Buddhism, namely, Zen.

As many artists know, a mountain of books have been written about the Zen of archery, gardening, motorcycle maintenance, drawing, and so on. Zen is a Japanese permutation of a Chinese school, called Chan, which takes its name from the Sanskrit *Dhyana* – all of which mean "meditation." Generally speaking, Zen ignores all of the metaphysical and even moral aspects of traditional Buddhism, and concentrates on meditative awareness. True meditative awareness is focused, in its purest form, on the *present* moment. Thinking about the past is a subjective construction (or imagining) of events that are already gone, and thinking about the *future* is also a subjective construction of nonexistent events. Pure meditation on the present moment can be done in a quiet cave someplace, but more important, it can be done actively – in the mundane activities of our daily life. Making tea, shoveling snow, cooking dinner, and so on can all become quite transcendent if we rigorously attend to the activity and refrain from thinking about the past and the future.

Anyone who's ever tried to "be here now" knows how odd and fresh an old, familiar activity becomes. Suddenly, you make a Zen shift and your basketball skills go into "the zone," or your garlic chopping gets strangely religious, or you lose yourself in playing a piano piece or doing a painting. Such moments are hard to attain, of course, but Zen led me to realize that mystical experiences didn't need to be drug-sparked, psychedelic blackouts of epic proportions. The present moment itself was a mystical wonder under my nose all the time. A transcendent experience is one in which we go beyond, or transcend, our usual self. But that doesn't mean we're having a metaphysical movement from this world to an eternal one, it just means we are having a meaningful state of extraordinary consciousness. Zen struck me as a wonderful alternative to the religious and metaphysical views about mystical experience.

I will explore the relationship between Zen and the arts in a separate chapter, but it's worth mentioning its importance here at the outset. Many people like myself come to Buddhism through the arts, because crafts, arts, and even meticulous chores can be expressions of spirituality. The secular and the sacred are collapsed in Zen, and that is a very attractive integration for many of us who are dissatisfied with the two-world thesis of most religions.

More important, I began to see that meditating on the present moment, even in small doses, was powerful medicine for much of the suffering in my teenage years. When we are older, teen angst looks pretty ridiculous. We look back at ourselves and have to shake our heads at the drama. Some of us became aggressive and bullied some innocent kid; some of us were bullied and plotted revenge fantasies; some of us fought against authority and ended up in the back of a squad car; some of us became suicidal over a derailed romance; some of us ran away because our parents were such "assholes"; some of us destroyed property, mutilated ourselves, or engaged in brutal catty politics. From a more mature vantage point, so much of this drama seems pointless and unnecessary. I remember obsessing about a girl so badly during my junior year that I thought I would lose my mind. And, like many other people who have had this experience, I was stupefied later when I realized how little I had in common with the object of my affection. It's astounding that we often develop infatuations with people whom we do not otherwise even *like* or *respect*. When the projected idealizations fade, we're dumbfounded by the original craving. All of this stuff looks silly to us in retrospect, but we have to remember that it was real suffering when it was happening. Buddhism appeals to many people because it focuses primarily on alleviating such human suffering.

We all know now that *time* heals most wounds and makes most slights seem ridiculous. But imagine if you didn't have to wait for five or ten years before you could laugh at your own misery. Imagine if you could do it while you were still gripped by the fresh pain – if you could emancipate yourself from the immediate weight of the hurt. Zen, and Buddhism generally, is a spiritual technology that allows one to get this soothing distance from suffering, even while the events are quite fresh. It does not create this freedom by consoling promises of another realm – on the contrary, it requires an even greater attention and commitment to this present experience, with its ephemeral, shifting, fluctuating aspect. The imaginative rehearsals of bully insults, prom rejections, bad grades, parental harangues, acne breakouts, social faux-pas, and all the other ingredients of teen angst can be shifted to our mental backburner while we focus on the now. With practice and discipline, this ability becomes stronger and more helpful. When more devastating pains eventually come our way, Buddhism can be a powerful antidote.

So, in summary, my own early path bumped along in a vaguely discernible direction. I was a disaffected teen, an outsider. I discovered the joys of ecstatic mystical experience – sometimes naturally, sometimes with controlled substances. This led me to a loosely Hindu philosophy of transcendentalism, one that celebrated peak-experiences as communions with an eternal divine reality. But this other-worldly transcendentalism slowly gave way to a more down-to-earth spiritualism the more I began to learn about Buddhism. Buddhism made me think that the solution to suffering is not to run away from, or escape, this world, but to run straight at it even harder.

Chapter II

Climbing the "Everest" of Cravings

Buddhism and Eros

Suffering arises from our disappointments. We think to ourselves: my wife is fat and I'm not attracted to her, my husband has a good body but he's an idiot, the girl I'm infatuated with won't be faithful, my boyfriend takes good care of me but has no sense of adventure, and so on. Our erotic confusions and frustrations seem endless.

The Buddha understood that erotic desire is one of the biggest challenges to achieving inner peace. Our obsession with beauty and the pleasures of the flesh is the major cause of ecstasy and misery. He asks us, in the *Mahadukkhakhandha Sutta* (13), to consider an ideal beautiful woman – he gives a list of traits: young, vital, of the noble class, not too tall or short, not too thin or fat, and so on. He says that this is the beautiful form/body in its absolute prime, and great pleasure and joy will accompany the woman herself and her devoted fan club of pursuers. The body itself can be understood as a player in a drama comprised of two acts: first, the allure or enchantment of body/form, and second, the disenchantment of body. Beauty fades. The Buddha suggests that we imagine this same beauty many years later, "sick, in pain, & seriously ill, lying soiled with her own urine & excrement, lifted up by others, laid down by others. What do you think: Has her earlier beauty & charm vanished, and the disenchantment occurred?" But a *third* act can be added to this sad plot by using the *dharma*. In the third act, one escapes from this toggling process altogether. By understanding that we tend to oscillate between attraction to beauty, disappointment, attraction, disappointment, attraction, and so on, we can begin to lighten up about the drama. "And what, monks, is the escape from forms? The subduing of desire-passion for forms, the abandoning of desire-passion for forms: that is the escape from form."

The escape is not from our feelings, in this case, our attractions and repulsions about the beautiful and the ugly. These levers and pulleys are part of having a body, a brain, a personality. They cannot be entirely removed, only transcended – in the sense that *wisdom* can recognize our own womanizing or femme fatale tendencies (or our fear of intimacy), and then *discipline* can diminish these obsessive components from our romantic lives. One of the reasons why I am a Buddhist is because it provides some kind of map, albeit imperfect, to the mysterious human heart.

The Chemistry of Romantic Desire

Fantasizing about the object of your desire can be a bitter-sweet obsession. It seeps into every other aspect of your life and flavors it with sometimes agreeable and oftentimes agonizing feelings. And on top of the psychological drama of erotic longing we must add the compulsions of our own *chemistry* to the equation. Saying that "love is chemical" is a well-worn cliché. But as neurobiology advances, the old cliché seems increasingly literal. Romantics and mystics everywhere resist the reduction of our "highest" emotions to mere chemical agitations. Maybe they're right to do so. But compelling data keeps streaming in about our true erotic triggers – pheromones, dopamine, norepinephrine, vaso-pressin, and oxytocin. Is my soul mate just the right bundle of biochemicals? Am I chemically determined to *imprint* on one kind of lover, rather than another? And if it's determined, then how can Buddhism (or anything else) possibly help to free me of such compulsion?

Look at your left hand. If your ring finger is slightly

longer than your index finger, then you probably got a little extra testosterone pumped into your system when you were just a developing fetus inside your mother. The finger size correlates with other masculine gender traits that hormones influence. Chemists and psychologists have correlated testosterone with personality traits like being analytical, exacting, competitive, hierarchic or rank-oriented, and narcissistic. Higher levels of estrogen, usually associated with women, are linked to being imaginative, creative, humane, sympathetic, and flexible (for more details, see Lori Gottlieb's "How Do I Love Thee," in *The Atlantic Monthly*, March 2006).

Internet dating services are actually trying to use information like the above to find good matches for searching singles. What people say they want in a partner and what they really want is not always the same (due to obvious social stigmas, and also the less acknowledged but equally important fact that people are often dishonest with themselves about what they like). Add to this problem the new insight that passionate romantic love has a very different set of chemicals associated with it than long-term bonding. The crush or infatuation (otherwise known as the lightning bolt) is correlated with high levels of dopamine in the brain, and the "honey, where's the remote?" and the "when are the grandchildren coming over?" longtermers have higher levels of oxytocin. Sometimes your chemicals are pushing you for immediate sexual gratification and sometimes your chemicals are pushing you for long-term stability (for women it's the "bad-boy versus nice guy" scenario, and for men it's the "femme fatale versus the house-frau" scenario that I sketched above).

Now add to this the fact that your genome is trying to reproduce itself with the most "fit" mate possible, because that will ensure a better immune system in your kids. Sometimes it seems that this unconscious genetic agenda is actually playing us like puppets in the realm of romance. For example, Professor Claus Wedekind of the University of Lausanne in Switzerland performed an experiment on forty-nine women. He asked the women to sniff sweaty t-shirts that had been worn by unidentified men and to rank their stench from best to worst (I'm not making this up – see Lauren Slater's article "Love," in *National Geographic*, February 2006). The test confirmed that women "preferred" the scent of men whose genotype was most different from their own – and diverse gene mixing is one proven way to make healthier babies. Unfortunately, the best baby-making partner (from the genetic point of view) is not always the best stable partner (from the childrearing compatibility point of view). Sometimes the intense sparks between lovers produces a child that has a strong *élan vital*, but then ironically those same sparks make the subsequent childrearing partnership very difficult.

Perhaps the most amazing data that's emerging from brain studies is the confirmation that love is a kind of *insanity*. According to a recent psychiatry study at the University of Pisa (see Slater, "Love"), the levels of serotonin (an important mood-related neurotransmitter) are very similar in lovers and obsessive-compulsive disordered patients. Both groups drop down 40 percent lower than normal healthy individuals. Erotic love is a kind of mental illness.

The idea that love is a kind of madness is obvious to anyone who's ever been in love. In Plato's *Phaedrus* he first denigrates love (eros) as a corrupting madness. The erotic drives, he suggests, are completely disruptive of the delicate psychological balance or harmony that makes up the "healthy" rational soul. Lovers are out of their minds. They are out of control – they are not themselves. After sketching the insanity of love and the slavery that flows from such self-alienation, Plato radically shifts the discussion to praise love. The erotic drive gets reinterpreted as the "wings of desire"and these wings are the means by which we humans rise above the mundane world to experience, if only briefly, the "higher realm." The process may be irrational and slightly out of control (like an unruly horse pulling your chariot) – but the intense energy of this drive is apparently necessary to lift us to such inaccessible heights. For Plato, love is a kind of insanity, but it is a form of ecstasy that reveals more truth to us than other forms of lunacy.

Despite Plato's ultimate praise for the erotic, most philosophical and religious traditions (particularly in the West) have sided more with his earlier disparaging assessments of eros. More often than not, desire has been characterized as an obstacle to, rather than a vehicle for, enlightenment. The history of Buddhism is also marked by hostile trends toward the body and its desires. The actual teachings of the Buddha take a *Middle Way* between giving in to eros (hedonism) and trying to annihilate it (ascetic hatred of the lust). But even Buddhism, as a cultural tradition, couldn't avoid falling back toward the extreme of asceticism.

Some later schools of Buddhism, like the Chinese Mind-Only school, emphasized a dualism of body versus mind. The physical world was thought to be illusion (*maya*), while the mental world was celebrated as the truly real. Bodily desires, like eros, were considered part of the illusory world, and must be ignored or rejected.

Asceticism seeks to mortify the flesh so that the spiritual dimension of the devotee will be purified or freed – even if only temporarily. For example, according to St. Augustine – who asked God to make him "chaste" but not just yet – the erotic drives are great obstacles to virtue. It is this basic presupposition, of the human soul as divided against itself, that leads the Eastern yogi to starve himself and deprive himself of sleep, and the Western priest and nun to refuse themselves erotic pleasures. To indulge the body, according to this tradition, is to give in to the "dark side." The early Christian presbyter Origen (184–254 CE) – who, incidentally, knew the Platonic *Dialogues* by heart – not only pronounced that his own body was alien to him, but also had himself castrated as a young man so that he might, without scandal, become a scripture teacher for females.

In order to best understand the Buddhist perspective on erotic desire and love, we have to fully grasp his Middle Way teaching. Sex is neither inherently wicked, as the ascetics argue, nor is it the summit of life, as the hedonists suggest. Let's follow the Buddha as he discovers, through meditation, the *dharma* of the Four Noble Truths. Then let's use his Middle Path logic to reflect further on love, sex, and craving. No philosopher, including the Buddha, has entirely unraveled the mysteries of erotic desire, but the *dharma* offers fresh perspectives for our constant struggle to manage our love lives.

A New Kind of Meditation

Sitting under the Bodhi tree, the Buddha used his meditation skills to enter into deeper and deeper trance states (*jhanas*). He had learned these techniques from Hindu ascetics during his days of wandering. He was a master of *jhana* meditation (*samadhi*), and found that he could move through different trance states with relative ease. First, sitting quietly and focusing on the breath as it moves in and out, the Buddha was able to quiet the mind and body. In this *jhana*, one detaches from the usual sense-desires and moves inward to watch the bubbling flow of thought itself. This first *jhana* is accompanied by feelings of delight and pleasure. From here, one moves to the second *jhana*, which is the cessation of thought itself. The constant discourse inside our mind, running like an incessant commentary on all experience, is finally silenced. When the inner blab finally shuts up, one has arrived in the second *jhana*. This trance state is still accompanied by a refined sense of delight and joy. But now, one is able to move to an even deeper level of concentration. In the third *jhana*, the more active feeling of joy (*piti*), which is like a form of rapture, evaporates and leaves behind only the awareness of happiness (*sukha*). Finally, even this *sukha* passes away and, in the fourth *jhana*, only the purest equanimity, empty awareness, remains. The mind has been utterly cleansed.

Samadhi meditation is a prized form of mental training in Buddhism because it gives greater powers of concentration to the practitioner. It also reveals the deficiency or conventionality of the usual subject/object (knower/known) distinction. In ordinary consciousness, we are always separate from the object of our experience – separated by words and labels (symbols and signs), separated by mental representations (ideas), and even separated by sensual representations (sense data impressions). *Jhana* meditation empties the mind of its usual representational activity, and gives the practitioner an awareness that is supposedly beyond the usual subject/object duality.

But for all that good stuff, *jhana* meditation was not the breakthrough technique for the Buddha. The problem with *jhana* meditation, according to Gautama, was that it did not have the practical insight (*vipassana*) to overcome the problem of suffering in our daily lives. *Jhana* meditation is a great head-trip, but we need something else to help find peace in our day-to-day lives.

Under the Bodhi tree, the Buddha switched from *jhana* meditation (*samadhi*) to his unique technique of mindfulness (*sati*). Mindfulness is a meditation on the impermanence of all things (*anicca*), but it is a systematic method. It proceeds sequentially through four domains: mindfulness of body (*kayanupassana*), mindfulness of feeling and sensation (*vedanupassana*), mindfulness of our conscious thinking patterns (*cittanupassana*), and mindfulness of our "mind objects" (i.e., our beliefs and ideas) (*dhammanupasanna*).

Each domain of mindfulness must be meditated in two modes, *internal* and *external*. For example, my body must be contemplated from the *inside* – I must become more aware of it in the present moment (its weight, shape, movement, and my own ability to calm or agitate the whole body). I must become mindful of the body's ever-changing aspect. But then, I must contemplate bodies generally (the external modality) by reflecting on their common nature. And what I find is that all bodies, my own and everyone else's, are slowly decomposing sacks of flesh, tissues, organs, and the like. The Buddha frequently describes the body as a repulsive "bag, with openings at both ends, filled with impurities." This is not because he hates the body per se, but rather because he wants to detach the normal clinging attitude that we usually have toward our bodies. Our own contemporary culture, for example, is obsessed with body image. We are surrounded by pictures of perfectly toned hard bodies on TV and in magazines, and the reigning question that American pop culture wants us to ask ourselves is, "Am I hot?" "Am I desirable?"

Young girls become bulimic and anorexic over this stuff. Young and not-so-young men are getting "thigh implants" and "pectoral implants" because their hours at the gym have failed to give them the "ripped" bodies they're after. Older folks are having themselves injected regularly with botulism in order to arrest the inevitable facial droop of aging. Skin is sliced, diced, and grafted, and fat is sucked out, while bones are broken and reset – all in pursuit of the urgent question, "Am I hot?"

The Buddha didn't know anything about these sci-fi technologies for prolonging the inevitable, but he understood very well that the human ego is tightly bound up and concerned with the body. Mindful meditation is designed to detach our ego from the body and to see it for what it is – an impermanent, composite thing that cannot avoid eventual breakdown. According to the *Mahasatipatthana Sutta*, a Buddhist should look at her body in a clinical, detached way. "Just as if a skilled butcher, having slaughtered a cow, were to sit with the carcass divided into portions, so a monk reviews his own body ... in terms of its elements." My body is made up of chemicals, like everything else, and these are capable of rearrangement into new forms or of eventual decay. "Again, a monk, as if he were to see a corpse in a charnel-ground, thrown aside, eaten by crows, hawks, or vultures, by dogs or jackals, or various other creatures, compares his own body with that, thinking: 'This body is of the same nature, it will become like that, it is not exempt from that fate.'"

How does this help with suffering? Isn't it just depressing to focus on my slow decomposition? At first it might seem like adding insult to injury, but meditating on your own impermanence is the way to liberate yourself from a common delusion. We suffer greatly, the Buddha thinks, because we want our bodies to last forever and to always be beautiful, but they cannot. We cling to our bodies because we are all craving for immortality. In doing so, we make the error of thinking that an inherently impermanent thing will last – a philosophical mistake in thinking. And we succumb to an unhealthy fantasy – a craving that we will live forever.

That day under the Bodhi tree, the Buddha expanded this rigorous mindful technique into the other domains besides the body. Our subjective feelings of pain and pleasure are also objects of our ego-craving tendencies. We seek to hold on to those feelings of bliss that come with intense pleasures like sex, food, drink, and even aesthetic pleasures. But we must, according to the Buddha, get a reality-check about these transient joys. Accept them for what they are, and even enjoy them. But don't obsessively chase after them in a state of denial about their fleeting nature. And just like one's feelings, one's mental tendencies must be analyzed and corrected – after all, the mind has narcissistic tendencies and ego-serving ways of operating. Each of us has his own particular neurosis and must engage in a detached and systemic meditation on his own unhealthy thinking patterns. And lastly, our beliefs, ideologies, and ideas can also fall prey to the clinging and attachment that mar other aspects of the human experience. Many of us cause tremendous misery to ourselves and others by our dogmatic allegiance to our beliefs. We make the same mistake – thinking that our ideas are perfect and permanent principles. We try to protect our pure incorruptible beliefs, and suffer when things change and the beliefs no longer seem coherent.

My grandmother, for example, was so attached to her Catholicism (and her wounded pride) that when her brother left the priesthood to marry a woman and be happy, she concocted a story and sustained it for decades. Because he moved out of state, she was able to tell friends and even relatives that he was doing the Lord's work as a missionary in Africa. She would not recognize his new family or otherwise interact with him anymore. And on a more serious note, one can see that radical Islam's suicide bombers seem to be neurotically attached to their beliefs about Islam – how else could they place those principles over the value of the flesh and blood that they leave in the streets and marketplaces? Buddhism suggests that a more realistic understanding of *belief* itself – one that's more flexible, revisable, and capable of evolution – will save us from the deep disappointments of punctured naiveté and the evil that we often enact on others. Experience should teach theory, not the other way around.

The Four Noble Truths

All this *mindful* meditation led the Buddha to a moment of beautiful clarity. He could see at once, sitting under the tree, how the problem of suffering could be solved. He attained enlightenment that day and crystallized his breakthrough in a formula, called the Four Noble Truths.

1. All life is suffering (*dukkha*).

2. All suffering is caused by craving (*tanha*).

3. Letting go of craving liberates us from suffering (*nibbana*).

4. The Eightfold Path is the way to let go of suffering.

To live is to suffer. This might seem a bit pessimistic, but the Buddha is simply stating that a variety of pains and misfortunes accompanies the human condition. For example, because we have a body, we are open to the suffering of degeneration (getting sick, growing old, etc.). Moreover, having family and friends means that we are all open to the pain of loss, disappointment, and even betrayal.

This somewhat depressing view is not merely the product of a melancholy disposition. The Buddha has a sophisticated psychological and biological interpretation of all this. The avenues by which these painful experiences travel – body, feeling, perception, disposition (will), and consciousness – are called the five aggregates (*khandas*). These five aggregates, or streams, converge together and make up our basic elements – each individual is composed of these basic components. They are the physiological and psychological faculties through which we both passively receive the world and actively partake in that world. The "person" or "self" is more identifiable with the aggregates, or "bundles of experience," than with a traditional "ghost in the machine" type of soul. These aggregates of experience are the "organs" of pleasure and pain, and it is in relation to pleasure and pain that human craving can begin to arise. The Buddha summarizes the First Noble Truth in the *Digha-Nikaya* scripture: "Birth is suffering; Decay is suffering; Death is suffering; Sorrow, Lamentation, Pain, Grief, and Despair are suffering; not to get what one desires is suffering; in short: the Five Aggregates of Existence are Suffering" (22).

The Second Noble Truth moves beyond the mere fact of human suffering to explore the *cause* of this unhappy condition. Suffering is caused by craving or attachment (*tanha*). The Buddha argues that sensations (sense data), like smells, sounds, tastes, bodily pleasures, and even the intellectual impressions (ideas), enter in through the aggregates and then inevitably give rise to craving. The sensual experiences themselves are not the causes of suffering, because they are inherently neutral. Instead, it's the response or attitude that we initiate after the sensation. Craving is a partly conscious, partly emotional, partly physiological "knee-jerk" that starts chasing the sensation after it has entered the system. For example, it's not the sensual experiences that money affords us – fine food, fancy clothes, travel, new cars, and the like – nor is it the material objects themselves that are inherently problematic. It's the craving (*tanha*), which becomes obsessed with repeating and sustaining those experiences, that actually causes the suffering – in this case, of greed. Suffering flows from the clinging attachment that mistakes *impermanent* things and sensations for lasting and *permanent* realities. Attachment or craving is a kind of confusion in the mind and the heart, one that tries to capture something that intrinsically can never be captured.

Pleasures certainly frustrate us and cause suffering because we remain overly attached to them, but why do we hang on to pains? Aren't we already in a hurry to get rid of these? It seems counterintuitive, at first, to say that we cling to our injuries. But further reflection makes it apparent. Indignation, for example, is one of the great culprits. When we feel indignant and personally injured or offended by some unpleasant sensations, we have mistakenly puffed ourselves up into an overly important thing. The ego holds on to all slights and nurses them until they're obese, overwhelming offenses. Moreover, there's a metaphysical point too. When we think of our self as injured, we have made the mistake that the traditional Hindus (and other religious thinkers) have made; namely, we have forgotten that we, too, are impermanent transitory realities. As an impermanent transitory reality, I can only be injured or indignant if I cling to myself, if I think of myself as a substance enduring through time. Craving, for the Buddha, is both an emotional passion and an intellectual misconception about reality. The suffering is caused when we falsely attribute "absolute" reality where there is only "relative" reality.

The Third Noble Truth states that the cure for suffering is nonattachment, or the termination of craving. Freedom is not the renunciation of all emotions and feelings, it's the ability to rise above the incoming sensations. You still feel pain and pleasure, but you no longer cling to these fluctuating experiences. In the *Dhammapada* scripture, Buddha explains: "The enlightened ones, at all times, surrender in truth all attachments. The holy spend not idle words on things of desire. When pleasure or pain comes to them, the wise feel above pleasure and pain" (83). Understanding and acting as if pleasures and pains are impermanent, like clouds forming and dissipating, leads to a liberation from our obsessions.

Well, it sounds good on paper. Now, how does one put it into practice? This leads to the Fourth Noble Truth. The cure for suffering, characterized in the Third Noble Truth as nonattachment, has eight steps or stages of practical realization, referred to as the Eightfold Path. The Eightfold Path is a set of prescriptive attitudes and activities that will lead to the extinction of suffering, it is the path of freedom. The path is divided up into three basic areas: ethical action (*sila*), mental training (*samadhi*), and wisdom (*panna*). In the *ethical* category, we find the sort of things one might expect: Right Speech, Right Action, and Right Livelihood (e.g., try not to lie, gossip, cheat, steal, have sex with other people's spouses, sell weapons, etc. – it's a manageable list for laypersons and a much longer one for monks). For *mental training*, we find Right Effort, Right Mindfulness, and Right Concentration (i.e., the methods for cultivating a powerful and disciplined mind). And for *wisdom*, we find Right View and Right Thought (i.e., the philosophy of impermanence and interconnection).

The Buddha's Middle Way was more than just a recipe for level-headed composure. It was the underlying secret, the solution to all suffering. There is a Middle Way between extreme actions, extreme lifestyles, and even extreme forms of thinking. The Eightfold Path tries to find that equilibrium in all the facets of human life.

Making Peace with the Body

Sexuality has a Middle Way, too. It is not a matter for absolute moral injunctions, but something more fluid and relative to individual people. This Middle Way path of Buddhism can be seen in the *Bhikkuni Sutta (Anguttara IV)*, where the monk Ananda, Gautama's righthand man, visits a nun who is ill. He honestly discusses the difficulties of living on the *dharma* path – the challenges of overcoming temptations and disciplining the mind. Ananda admits to the nun that, paradoxically, food is how we can actually *overcome* food. And here he means that eating moderately when we're hungry is the best way to forget about food – to overcome our cravings for food. Anybody who's ever gone on an extreme diet knows that starving yourself is a practice that tends to put food at the forefront of your consciousness. It becomes hard to concentrate on anything *but* food. Similarly, Ananda says that sometimes conceit is the way to overcome conceit. For example, a young traveler on the *dharma* path may see the freedom and equanimity of a more experienced monk, and say to himself, "Well, if he can do it, so can I." And so an immature feeling may lead, like a catalyst, to greater effort, resolve, and the real attainment of inner peace. In this context of realism about our desires, Ananda mentions that sexual intercourse must be overcome if we are to achieve real peace. And the nun suddenly confesses that she has been weak in this area (her own regret has now made her ill). Ananda gives the confession a light response, suggesting to the woman that she just get over it and move on. Everybody makes mistakes.Live and learn. The nun is hugely relieved and returns to health.

This realism about erotic drives augured a later development in Buddhism, namely, Tantric Buddhism. Is it possible to overcome sex by having sex? Well, sign me up for that brand of spirituality! Of course, a lot of brow-raising and jokes have grown up around the idea of Tantric sex. But the philosophy is straightforward. Once you've ceased despising the body and accepted it as another aspect of your being (i.e., valueneutral, impermanent, inevitable), then you can use it (just like you use the mind) to transcend ego tendencies and experience ecstatic *anatta* (no-self). You and your partner, in the protracted "little death" of orgasm, can transcend the subject/object dichotomy.

Celestial sex is well and good, if you find yourself in a relationship of mutual attraction, good chemistry, trust, compassion, and nonneurotic partnership. But what about the 99 percent of the rest of us? Yes, one solution to healing the insanity of love is actually finding someone who reciprocates all that heat, and who also miraculously provides stability, security, and refuge. This miraculous combination appears regularly on TV and in movies, but it proves largely truant in the real world.

A Cultural Divorce of Partnership and Passion

Another solution, one that I have seen many times in Buddhist countries, is to separate romance from marriage. I'm not recommending this practice, but simply acknowledging it as one more effective strategy in the reduction of erotic suffering. In the West, we assume that erotic romance is supposed to lead eventually to partnership and family.

Historically speaking, this assumption is a recent invention (even in the West), but it is definitely not the way in Asia (or most of the developing world). Contrary to the "love marriages" of the West, the "arranged marriages" of the East are more successful – as measured by divorce rates anyway. Of course, we have to acknowledge that in some countries women's economic reliance on men also contributes strongly to the low divorce rates and it has nothing to do with philosophical reasons.

Nonetheless, one recognizes, in this system, a very effective strategy for raising children (and the purpose of marriage in this system is the raising of children). You do not look for the man or woman who sends electricity up your spine and leaves you panting and swooning. You look for a good provider, or healthy caretaker, with a modicum of prosperity and a capacity for devotion. When you're going to get married, you look for somebody who's got your back, so to speak. Many men and women, then, are devoted to social monogamy, but this doesn't always entail sexual monogamy.

Having lived in Asia, I see a kind of pragmatic Buddhism at work in this system. Buddhism says, do not have desires, expectations, assumptions about the world and then wait for the world to conform to them. That is a recipe for disaster. Instead, we should examine and accept the way the world is, and have our expectations conform to that. Suffering comes, in part, from the disappointments that follow our unrealistic expectations.

Understanding that we have some motives within us that are often working at cross-purposes can help us reduce some suffering. Some forces within us are driving us toward safety, security, and stability, while others are pushing us toward danger, chaos, and adventure. To expect one person to actually embody all these qualities, when and where we want them (since we are constantly oscillating ourselves), is a ridiculous expectation. And getting more clarity about one's own goals can reduce suffering as well.

Having some beautiful girl or pretty boy on your arm may make you feel important, give you a status boost, or just be intrinsically fun, but these pleasures should not guide your decisions about a childrearing partner. It's like a farmer having a joy-ride in a Lamborghini, and then thinking it will do a good job plowing his soybean field. And vice versa, one cannot expect the strong, dependable co-parent of your kids to strut around the house like a Victoria's Secret model. That would be great, I admit. And I'm not going to take it off my fantasy list. But I'm not really confused about the different goals of my relationships – the different pleasures and purposes, the different means and ends.

Notice again that in Buddhism the different experiences themselves are value-neutral – it is not better to be a family man than a swinging bachelor, a career woman than a mother. It is not intrinsically better to date house-fraus than femme fatales. The suffering comes from (1) mixing up the expectations (about the purposes, pleasures, and forms of happiness) that these different paths produce and (2) forgetting the impermanent nature of all these experiences.

Romance is a perfectly legitimate source of happiness, as is a lifestyle of service, or family duty, or a reflective life of scholarly pursuit, or whatever. And one person can pursue all of these in different chapters of her life. But clear-eyed analysis suggests that some of these life choices rule out others, at least for a time. You cannot be a good parent *and* be gone all the time. You cannot betray your lover and simultaneously expect the benefits of monogamy. You cannot date a boy and expect him to be a man. Wisdom suggests that we accept these mutual exclusions with some grace and even good cheer. After all, since everything is impermanent, then one is not trapped in a lifestyle choice forever. But when you're in whatever path, for whatever length of time, then you must strive to be truly present in it.

Wisdom in romance is crucial, of course, and while it doesn't always have to wait until we're older to make its appearance in our lives, it certainly can be found more readily in the older population. Divorce rates, for example, are illuminating when one looks at age breakdowns. We all know that half of marriages end in divorce, but it is remarkable how much age matters to the statistics. The divorce rate for couples who marry under the age of 24 is very high – around 37 percent. The figure almost cuts in half when you look at the 25- to 29-year-old range – around 18 percent. And it halves again between 30 and 34, and, astonishingly, the divorce rates for couples who marry in their late 30s is down around 6 percent. This makes sense to me because detachment (the ability to roll with the punches) increases with age for most people. Keeping your cool is literally a Buddhist virtue, since nirvana means "cooling off" or extinguishing a flame. The *dharma* is a way of attaining this cool, no matter what age you find yourself.

Power Politics and the War of the Sexes

The throes of passion might dissipate as we move into the autumn of our years, but until we're completely cooled-off (and possibly in the cold ground) we're going to be entangled on some front of the "war of the sexes." The war is probably as old as sexual dimorphism – as old as evolution's separation of male and female.

Sexual conflict can be quite extreme and even cause antagonistic evolutionary changes in a species. For example, male bean weevils have evolved spiny genitalia that allow them to fasten onto females and deliver more sperm, but this can damage the female (reducing her fitness) and so she has evolved a countermeasure. She kicks relentlessly at the male during copulation, and this reduces the possibility of her injury. Or consider the gamergate ants, whose females capture a male and snip off his genitals during copulation. They discard the male's body, but his severed genitals continue to fertilize for an hour. Thankfully, we humans don't have it this bad.

Animals, especially mammals, have ended up with different genitals, different brains, and different agendas. Add to these biological and psychological cross-purposes the cultural and social innovations that derail human monogamy, and it's easy to see why so much suffering comes with the romantic territory. It is exceedingly difficult to forge and sustain strong relationships.

Maybe it's some bias on my part, but it seems like relationships were more stable in my parents' generation. I'm not naive. I'm sure some of this "success" was the result of pre-liberation women just resigning themselves to disempowered lives of quiet married desperation. But men, too, seemed to have a greater resignation about the difficult selfless work that partnership demanded. My generation seems to throw in the towel earlier than the previous generation.

I'm not some conservative moralizer, preaching from on high. I've been divorced twice. I'm just trying to find my way through it all, like everybody else. For me, Buddhism has been a useful strategy for handling my own romantic suffering because it searches the heart and mind for unhealthy patterns of desire, analyzes their origins and their flexibility, and then tries to reeducate them. Buddhism is not a panacea, but it is a formidable remedy to include in our pharmacy of tonics.

German philosopher Arthur Schopenhauer once said, "The final aim of all love intrigues, be they comic or tragic, is really of more importance than all other ends in human life. What it all turns upon is nothing less than the composition of the next generation ... . It is not the weal or woe of any one individual, but that of the human race to come, which is here at stake." Charles Darwin even quoted this passage, approvingly, in his famous discussion of human animality in *The Descent of Man*.

Despite Schopenhauer's and Darwin's claim that it is not the "weal and woe of any one individual" that is at stake, it sure *feels* like that's the issue when your own heart is being torn asunder. But we have all come to appreciate, especially after Darwin and Sigmund Freud, that there are indeed motives at work inside us that we do not always recognize or acknowledge in the conscious mind. The Buddha, however, grasped this insight long before the Victorians. The reason why Buddhism is often considered a psychological theory, rather than a religion, is that it recognizes the huge role that hidden thoughts and emotions play in our own unhappiness. Isolating our own pathologies and retraining our minds can free us from some unnecessary suffering.

Everyone's familiar with the old saying that "power corrupts." But power obsession is not restricted to money. Men, for example, can be pigs about sexual conquest, notching their belts and ignoring the consequences of their quest for dominance. In many cases, men are blissfully ignorant of their own damaging tendencies – the hidden thoughts and emotions that play a role in their own and their partner's unhappiness. Women, however, have their own egoistic pursuits and power trips. Beauty is, after all, a kind of power.

"Women are everywhere conscious of the value of their own beauty," Darwin asserts, "and when they have the means, they take more delight in decorating themselves with all sorts of ornaments than do men." Is this sexist? Maybe.

Darwin gives the ultimate power to women, however, when he points out that the fairer sex actually creates and shapes the evolution of the male, because women usually decide with whom they want to sleep and with whom they want to mix their DNA. Women control the mating dance. Men perform all manner of attention-getting moves, but women decide which of the performing monkeys gets to pass on their genes.

Women may or may not be calculating complex benefits and risks when they evaluate partners – Does he have broad shoulders? Is he well-educated? Is he tall? Does he have a big bank account? Does he love Jesus? And so on. But almost every guy I know is comparatively one-dimensional in his visual attraction to women. Is she beautiful? This question trumps almost all others.

How male and female desire manifests is crucial data for a Buddhist approach to romance. Before any level of freedom can be achieved, Buddhism needs to know what specific cravings are taking root in the psyche and why. I will operate on my admittedly controversial assumption that men crave sexual union more narrowly (like a musician who only knows one song), while women seek power over a wider range of social economics. This is not a value judgment or assumption. Yes, craving is a bad thing in Buddhism, but one gender does not crave more than another – they simply distribute their cravings over different territory.

The Original Attachment

One explanation of the different craving patterns comes from standard twentieth-century developmental psychology. The Buddha would not have recognized the language of contemporary developmental psych, but his own approach is its true precursor.

Bonding is totally different for men and women because our original bonding experiences with our mothers (the first bonds) were different. In the beginning, we are all close to our mothers – so close, in fact, that we don't even know that we're *different* from our mothers. Little baby boys and girls don't even have egos yet, and their sense of *self* actually includes the mother (after all, she was transferring nutrition and warmth to you for many months while you were in the *nirvana*-like bliss of the uterus). The first indication that you're *not* in paradise anymore and that you're different from your mom is when (postumbilical bliss) you're hungry and her breast milk is not immediately in your face. Horror of horrors, you're not that God-like everything you thought you were back in the womb. But over time, you begin to relish your newfound ego and start to exercise it regularly – trying to figure out its limits and powers. Self-formation only happens by distancing your self from the big warm host (mom) whom you've been parasitically merged with for so long.

Little girls have to psychologically take *one* step away

from the mother, detaching themselves from her and recognizing that they are individuals. They have to figure out, "Okay, I'm *not* my mother." Everybody has to make this step of detachment in order to be a vaguely functioning human being. Boys have to take an additional step. They first detach from mom in the same way girls do, but then at some point they have to figure out: "Okay, I'm not my mother … *and* I'm not even the same *kind* of thing as my mother. I've got this thing between my legs and I appear to be more like that scruffy creature over there reading the newspaper and scratching his ass." Boys must detach *two* positions from the mother, while girls only have to move one position. This detachment survives into later life, making guys more remote and objective, while women are generally more attached, subjective, and nurturing.

Almost a whole century of people lying on the analyst's couch has made us familiar with the idea that the romance in our later life has hidden connections to our earlier life. In our adult lives we all want to join with another person, and the *ideal* joining or bonding is the memory of our original bond – back when all our desires and needs were met by the Uber-partner, mom. Interuterine bliss was the closest thing that anybody gets to full satisfaction (no cravings, or more accurately, precravings).

Later in life many lovers subconsciously want their mates

to be their everything, their end-all be-all, their one and only, their protector, their provider, their teddy-bear, and so on. Many people have heard the treacly sweet "He *completes* me!" And sometimes "needy" men (i.e., mama's boys, to use the vernacular) will be equally stifling in their approach.

Women (and men too) feel a little bit broken after that original unity with the mother, so they spend their lives trying to re-create a little bit of that unity with subsequent lovers. But since men are more detached in general, they tend to be regular disappointments to the female desire for a more smothering kind of union. Women are better *connected* to other humans than men are. But the downside of being better connected is that women's urge for union (or possession) is sort of absolute – it recognizes few boundaries. For men, the urge for union with another is momentary – the sex act is pretty much sufficient for quashing the urge. Guys get their fill of completion fairly quickly. When men continually fail to complete their partners in all the other emotional aspects of life, women turn to more nurturing possibilities, like other women, romance novels, and cats.

Buddhism recognizes the tragic nature of these masculine and feminine desires – they both want what is literally impossible. Sex is great but it is intrinsically fleeting. Likewise, complete emotional merging is also impossible. As goals for our romantic desires, both of these are probably neurotic. They are causes of unnecessary suffering. A Buddhist metaphysics, which reminds us of the impermanence of such pleasures, and a Buddhist psychology, which reminds us of our confused mental habits, can help to balance our usual romantic missteps.

Buddhism and the Broken Heart

Perhaps the one greatest source of romantic suffering is also the most difficult to cure. Yes, we are tormented by our own conceptual confusions and crossed-wires of emotion, but we really just want one painful riddle solved: Why doesn't the other person love me back? The broken heart is unparalleled in the arsenal of misery. The answer to the riddle is usually complicated but even if you could identify the true reason for unreturned affection, it would be cold comfort. In this chapter we've seen some of the dizzying variables in romance: timing, age, chemicals for stability, hormones for danger, psychoanalytic gender formation, power trips, social stigma, immunological compatibility, and so on, ad infinitum. If you've imprinted onto somebody and that person hasn't imprinted back, then you have to resign yourself to a lengthy, but mercifully finite, detour of pain. You cannot control the other person's feelings. That's why Buddhism focuses on your own feelings, which you can scarcely control as well – but at least here you've got a fighting chance.

Buddhism redirects us to our own psyche to untangle the mess. Some universal tangles will need work – like the tendency to attach to our feelings (craving). But also some *particular* (nonuniversal) psychological patterns will need work (e.g., an abusive parent can leave a mark on our much later romantic pursuits, or a selfish person can use and discard lovers, or fear can cripple a person's social skills, or whatever). Even the moth-to-the-flame craziness of eros has its own inner logic – partly psychological, partly physiological. Our Buddhism, as a method of liberation, must pursue these psycho-physiological facts. The Buddha did what he could with the relatively rudimentary science of his day, but we have even more tools at our disposal to continue the *dharma* work. Buddhism encourages us to change those psycho-physiological patterns that we can and to *accept* those we cannot.

The refreshing aspect in all this is that Buddhism aligns with the sciences here, not the religions. Praying to Jesus or Allah to help me with my romantic suffering is, comparatively, like throwing money into a fountain. It might make you feel good for a moment, but it won't address the root causes of romantic suffering. A Buddhist may go to a temple and make offerings and even entreat the gods for help – everybody, myself included, can get so desperate that they'll try anything. But technically speaking, Buddhists go to a temple to take the *Three Refuges*. The *Triple Gem*, or Three Refuges of Buddhism, refer to (1) the Buddha himself, (2) the dharma, or teachings, and (3) the Buddhist community (*sangha*). Buddhists will focus on these three things to help them concentrate their minds on the difficult work of detachment. They don't expect the Buddha to hear their prayers and then rearrange the universe in their favor. After all, if we're suffering from a romantic crisis, what do we really expect Jesus, or Allah, or Guan Yin to do for us? "Dear Jesus, can you please make the other person love me back"? That seems patently juvenile. In fact, I suspect that most religious prayers regarding romantic suffering are requests for inner peace and freedom. "Please let this pass quickly." Buddhism seeks the same goal of equanimity, but pursues *causes* rather than *favors*. Those root causes will be found inside you, not outside.

Chapter III

A Natural Exercise in No-Self

Buddhism and Parenting

My interest in Buddhism, during my teens and 20s, was largely academic and conceptual. It seemed like a philosophically rigorous system, with compelling metaphysical ideas. Early on, it fed a Romantic bohemian need in me, and this was a fairly self-absorbed study of my own alienation. Becoming a father, however, forced me to reevaluate and reapply my Buddhism. Yes, the abstract contemplations were great, but as a father ... I needed *help!* I needed some strong medicine on a daily basis.

Raising my son, now 6 years old, has been the most exhausting, stressful, and beautiful mess I've ever experienced. I have not played the usual role of the absentee father, working nine-to-five. Instead, I have been the principal caregiver to my son. This means that my parenting experience has been more like the average mother's experience, in the sense that I spent every waking moment with my boy until, sweet merciful Jesus, he went to kindergarten. The upside of this bonding is so powerful that I will not even try to express it, but let's just say that we are very close.

Many parents these days, scrambling to balance career and family, will talk of spending "quality time" with their kids. I don't really know what this means. I guess it means that the time spent together is short, but somehow it's deeper and richer than regular old time. When I see parents and kids spending quality time together, they look exhausted by the sheer effort to be deeper and richer. Usually it entails racing the kids from one personal development chore to another. We don't believe in quality time in my family – we just do a lot of "quantity time."

Of course, I did all the exhausting work necessary for all babies: changing diapers, feeding, dressing, cleaning, playing, tending to fevers and colds, and so on. But when my son, who was always extremely spirited, started to crawl and walk and talk, I thought it would get easier, and it only got harder. This work was doubly exhausting because I did most of it alone.

My boy was so curious, fearless, and fast, that I spent the lion's share of my day just keeping him alive. I became convinced that my toddler son was trying to kill himself –

and *sometimes* I felt obliged to stop him. This may sound cruel and callous to the ears of nonparents, but those of us enrolled in the offspring management program will sigh in acknowledgment. My son's own death or dismemberment seemed chief among his otherwise indecipherable projects. He was always busy with it. According to my field notes, experiments, and round-the-clock observations, he seemed to prefer causing himself blunt traumas, but in a pinch he was not averse to corrosive solvents or poisons, if they were ready to hand.

Before I procreated my spawn, I would enter a home, or a park, or a public space with barely a register on my pulse. Perhaps I noticed the decorative aesthetic of a friend's house, or the clever architecture of a building lobby, or the landscaping of a public garden. If it wasn't a pleasant experience, it was certainly no worse than neutral. But as the father of an extremely energetic toddler, I was filled with dread and worry every time I went from one unfamiliar room to another – usually chasing after him as he bolted ahead. I was constantly assessing the potential injury and mortality quotient of every new space. This might strike some people as excessively worrisome, but all I can say is, you don't know my son.

Before I was a parent, I never imagined how many ways a kid can possibly injure himself in the average shopping mall, backyard, kitchen, or bathroom. But here I was, entering every new room with a lightning-fast security scan of stairs, cutlery, sharp sculptures, fragile artwork, heavy bookcases, tempting electrical outlets, anything glass, reachable electronic devices, choking hazards, and myriad other dangers. I knew with absolute certainty, like I know 2 plus 2 equals 4, that my son would go for every one of these deadly possibilities. If you filled an airplane hangar with fluffy pillows, stuffed animals, and safe plastic toddler toys, but you buried a pair of scissors at the far end somewhere, he'd have them in hand in under five minutes.

I offer a description of just one, randomly chosen, ten-minute episode with my son to try to convey the kind of constant *damage control* that all parents do. I had to take my son to work one afternoon, because the babysitter fell through at the last minute. At my office, I tried to set up my 2-year-old on a DVD cartoon show, just to keep him distracted for fifteen minutes while I did some computer work. While I was putting the DVD into the machine, my son climbed to the top of his chair and tried to jump across the room to land on my back – a physically impossible span for even the best athlete. He made it halfway and landed with a thud on the floor, where he rolled around with the wind knocked out of him. When I finally wiped away the last of his tears, I cut up an apple for us to eat. He immediately dropped his piece on the floor, where it picked up a wayward staple that had been hiding in the carpet. I caught the deadly apple slice just before he popped it in his mouth. While I, now sweating, was removing the staple from the apple and simultaneously missing an important phone call, he was serenely filling his diaper. After removing his copiously soiled diaper, I turned to find him somehow standing, now naked, at the top of the chair again – ready to launch.

Thankfully, some of this stress is dissipating as my boy gets older. He seems less bent on testing his invincibility complex, but, of course, new parenting worries rise up to replace the old ones. The Buddha tells us that practicing *mindfulness* will attune us to the present moment and give us peace, equanimity, and liberation from suffering. But can I "mindfully" harass my son to eat his breakfast every morning? Can I remain detached while he recklessly endangers himself and others throughout the day? Can I sustain equanimity while he escapes from the bath and runs naked around the house? Or stay cool and Buddha-like when he suddenly tells the large guy in from of us on the subway that said guy is "too fat" and "should not eat so much"?

There are docile children, who give their parents very little grief. But my son's mother and I didn't make one of those children. In my experience, raising a child has been like having a miniature war under our roof. Quiet contemplative meditation seems like a very remote luxury to me. I fantasize about joining a monastery and letting wolves raise my son instead. But then, what good is my Buddhism if it can't handle the chaos of everyday life?

Bohemian Buddhism

On the face of it, it's hard to see the Buddhist angle for parenting and familial love generally. Didn't Gautama leave his whole family to search for philosophical wisdom? As I mentioned before, Buddhism has always been attractive to bohemian culture. Jack Kerouac and other *dharma* bums like Gary Snyder and Allen Ginsberg all found a new intellectual platform for their counterculture explorations of consciousness. Kerouac even wrote his own version of the Buddha's biography. In the 1970s, Buddhist teacher Chogyam Trungpa appealed to radicals with his message of "crazy wisdom" – encouraging devotees to throw off the repressions of societal expectation. And, of course, the freethinking cartoon radical Lisa Simpson, who regularly challenges the status quo of Springfield, is a self-proclaimed Buddhist. But Buddhism itself was bohemian long before there were bohemians.

When he was 30 years old Gautama left his family and society, and, like other wanderers, floated around without the constraints of career and kin. Jesus did the same thing, as did St Anthony, St. Francis of Assisi, and Gandhi. Eccentric antisocial behavior seems interlaced with spiritual ambition.

Eventually, the Buddha discovered that his ascetic behaviors, inspired in part by Hindu and Jain mendicants, only led to more suffering. He tried fasting, giving away all his property, and denying himself all pleasures. In the end, he almost starved to death and had to be rescued from the Ganges River because he didn't have the strength to bathe himself.

After his experiments with privation and destitution, Gautama hit upon the Middle Way (*madhyama pratipad*) – a path of moderation between the extremes of austerity and opulence. Money cannot help you escape suffering, but neither can severe self-denial. After he gave up punishing himself, he cultivated a healthier mind and body, and in this healthier state he sat down beneath a fig tree (later called the Bodhi tree) to solve the riddle of suffering.

Buddhism, as an approach to life, always looks for *balance* as its ideal. But even its own history is marked by pendulum swings, doctrinal disputes, and sectarian tendencies. Without getting into the mind-boggling myriad schools of Buddhism, we should at least recognize – from the Four Noble Truths on down – that Buddhism has always been interested in two major areas: *ethics,* and *consciousness.* These two interests can be married together, and *should* be according to the Buddha, but even a cursory examination of history reveals that they often diverged and took turns dominating the imaginations of individuals and nations.

Buddhism itself, when considered historically, might be considered as a kind of bohemian counterculture traveler. At its birth, it came kicking and screaming against dominant Hindu society. But even when it traveled north into China and south into Sri Lanka, it came up against entrenched hierarchic indigenous ideologies. Buddhism arrived like a rebellious young punk in a China that was already dominated by a conservative Confucian philosophy. Though Kongzi (Confucius) and Gautama were contemporaries, Buddhism (Fojiao) didn't really enter China for another six or seven hundred years, and when it did, it found a rich intellectual culture that had no particular truck with meditation or individual enlightenment. To Confucian culture, Buddhism (brought from Central Asia) seemed amoral and antithetical to the family-based social structure of China. For the Chinese, the business of *ethics* was already firmly in hand, so Chinese Buddhism tended to stress its other major interest – *consciousness*. Even here it had a tough road, albeit eventually successful. Confucius himself, in the *Analects* (XV.31), offers a humorous assessment of holy men who spend their days in meditation. Preferring book-learning to meditation, Kongzi says, "I once spent all day thinking without taking food and all night thinking without going to bed, but I found that I gained nothing from it. It would have been better for me to have spent the whole time in *learning*."

Buddhism seemed to most Chinese to be a species of their own homegrown bohemia, namely, Daoism. Arguably, Chan/Zen Buddhism took as much, if not more, from Daoism – which celebrated the natural world over the social. Zen and Daoism emphasized individualism and mystical attunement. They were not particularly helpful in mundane matters like the family and the state. Zhuangzi, the famous Daoist philosopher, was fishing on the P'u River when the prince of Ch'u sent some officials to see him and said, "Our prince desires to burden you with the administration of the Ch'u state." Zhuangzi went on fishing without turning his head and said, "I have heard that in Ch'u there is a sacred tortoise which died when it was three thousand years old. The prince keeps this tortoise carefully enclosed in a chest in his ancestral temple. Now would this tortoise rather be dead and have its remains venerated, or would it rather be alive and wagging its tail in the mud?" "It would rather be alive," replied the two officials, "and wagging its tail in the mud.""Begone!"cried Zhuangzi."I too will wag my tail in the mud." So, Buddhism found a kindred spirit in Daoism's antisocial philosophy, but it must be recognized that Confucian conservatism comprised the mainstream Chinese majority.

Buddhism has usually come into a new region as a

heterodox and exotic import. In Japan it encountered a sophisticated high culture of Shintoism, in Tibet it crashed into the indigenous animism of Bon, in Southeast Asia it struggled for dominance with a longstanding Brahminism. During certain eras, Buddhism certainly became what we might call the status quo (e.g., imperial patronage made Buddhism a state religion), but the more mystical tint of later Buddhism (Mahayana) always ensured some bohemian credibility.

However, despite all of these maverick beatnik tendencies in the cultures of Asia, Buddhism still contains a surprising amount of wisdom about ordinary family life. The emphasis on consciousness, meditation, and mental training has certainly flourished in Western versions of Buddhism, so it may seem surprising that the *dharma* has application to family, friends, career, and so on. But the ethical dimension is there from the very start, under the Bodhi tree, and still informs Buddhist cultural life in Asia. Let's look at some of the ways that Buddhism can be applied in the domain of familial love.

The Lotus Sutra, the Six Perfections, and the Realities of Modern Parenting

In the *Lotus Sutra*, we find six domains of life that Buddhists must try to develop. They are called the Six Perfections (*paramitas*). They are derivative of the Eightfold Path, which makes up the Buddha's Fourth Noble Truth. In my attempt to apply my Buddhism to parenting, I have tried to keep the *paramitas* in mind. The First Perfection is the *Dana paramita*, which means generosity and giving of oneself. Every parent knows about this very intimately. Buddhism, contrary to Hindu philosophy, believes that there is no real "self" inside us – we don't have some essential soul that we're trying to protect or perfect. To imagine that we do have some important core self will distract us, according to the Buddha, from the selfless activity of generosity. One of the most obvious ways to actualize the no-self doctrine (*anatta*) in your life is to give that life in service – a daily but powerful gift that most parents understand perfectly well. When you become someone's parent, you pick up something that you can never really put down again.

The late, great Thai Buddhist monk Buddhadasa Bikkhu pointed out that our usual way of operating and functioning in the world is characterized by me-and-mine consciousness. What's in it for me? Parenting effectively ends that mode of consciousness, and shifts it to the no-self mode. Dedicating yourself to something or someone takes you out of your me-and-mine modality. And, according to Buddhism, serving your child, or your elderly parent, or some needy person is more helpful than serving some God. After all, even if there *is* a perfect being, he certainly doesn't need your help as much as these people do.

The Second Perfection is *Sila paramita*, which means morality, or proper conduct. This includes things like Right Speech, Right Livelihood, and Middle Way moderation in all things. I fail regularly in this area, and I always have. But when you have a child, whose very character is largely in your hands, you begin to understand the need to display your better self. And to do it sincerely, as much as possible. Your kid, the walking, talking sponge, is watching you carefully at all times.

Recently, my son asked his playmate, "What is your fuckin' problem?" And I realized, yet again, that I have to attend more to my own Right Speech.

Right livelihood is an interesting aspect of the *Sila paramita* because it asks us to think about our career choices as moral choices – something rarely considered in capitalist-consumerist cultures like our own. Yes, I want my son to be successful and have the prosperity necessary for travel and the "finer things" in life, but I don't want him to make a living by exploiting other people. If he comes to make his living by deceiving people, then I will be ashamed. We all console ourselves with the sop of "buyer beware" (caveat emptor), and so much exploitation is everywhere in advertising, sales, investment, and labor that we've become numb to the moral

[handwritten note:] noe was regardless of occupation there is still some exploitation (indirectly or your sons orchard) - even vegans may contribute to exploitation of crop farmers?

implications. But I do not want my son to make a living by violence or deceit. Not because God will see it and punish him, or because his soul will be stained. Rather, this kind of mendacity, an expression of bad character, seeps like a poison into all of one's dealings with people – including the more "sacred" relations (family and friendship) – the relations that nourish our humanity. I don't want my son to be a smarmy, unctuous person. I want him to have integrity. And that means that I have to be modeling integrity on a daily basis, as much as I can. God ... I mean Buddha, help me!

The Third Perfection is *Ksanti paramita*, which means patience and endurance. Parenting affords at least ten tests of this *paramita* every single day. The cuteness, beauty, sweetness, lovability, adorability, delightfulness,and charm of children are regular topics of conversation, but almost no one mentions how dumb they are. Of course, they all catch up eventually, and mine will no doubt surpass me quickly, but it's also true that for a while they're dumb as squirrels. The transmission of knowledge (skills, basic logic, facts, language, etc.) is your job as parent. Nobody can do it but you. Some parents are naturally patient and can repeat some basic training exercise over and over again, without any ill effects on the blood pressure. I'm not one of them. But I'll be damned if I let my son see my frustrations. It's not his fault that he can't walk at 6 months, or wipe his ass at 10 months, or tie his shoe at 3 years old, or sit still through an opera, or eat with chopsticks, or understand Hegel, or whatever. It's ludicrous to get impatient over these things, but it's also insincere to pretend that we don't get impatient. After watching my son trying to put on his gloves for twenty minutes, I am frustrated. I'm not going to pretend that I'm not. But patience and endurance are about *mastering* your emotions, not eliminating them. Feeling frustrated is part of having psycho-physiological equipment, but it is in my power to check myself and restrain myself. So I will.

Here's a fact that I learned as a parent: little boys cannot sit still. They really *cannot* sit still. They know perfectly well *how* to do it, and they might even *want* to do it. But a 4-year-old boy can no more sit still than he can grow a beard. His own biology, percolating with testosterone, makes all docile behavior impossible. Is this a generalization? Of course. There are many exceptions to this rule, but my point is that some discernable facts about a boy's physiology and psychology can be ascertained – facts that seem like pathologies at first, but really just follow necessarily from the nature of chemistry and brain function. According to Andrew Sullivan's article, "The He Hormone," the physiological differences between the sexes are striking at an early age. At the outset, girls are much better-adjusted human beings than boys, though the latter eventually catch up. "Ninety-five

[handwritten margin note: book is too specific to parenting of a young male child / toddler.]

percent of all hyperactive kids are boys; four times as many boys are dyslexic and learning-disabled as girls. There is a greater distinction between the right and left brain among boys than girls, and worse linguistic skills."

Once I realized that it was in fact normal for my son to leap around like a psychotic jumping bean, then I outgrew my own anxiety about it and I also developed a better parenting technique – one that involved less yelling, less spanking, and less unrealistic demands. Some may say that this is only commonsense wisdom, and, yes, that is all Buddhism is saying too. But such parental realism and adaptability are harder to master than one might imagine. For example, many people cannot seem to align the *reality* of their child with the fictional *idea* of their child, and subsequently spend untold energy trying to force an impossible procrustean fit. Or they try to "medicate" their child into a more manageable version.

The Dutch/Jewish philosopher Baruch Spinoza (1632–1677) offered a very Buddha-like theory (despite having never heard of the Buddha) of human happiness through intellectual enlightenment. In his famous *Ethics* (part V), he says that when the mind comes to understand the real causes of things – how some things could not have been otherwise and simply lie outside the realm of our control – then we cease to worry and fret over them. Nature and the human psyche have normal propensities and tendencies, and if we're not attuned to these, we will be anxious that things are not as they should be. Imagine if some alien race came to Earth, for the first time, and took stock of the human species. They should no doubt be horrified and feel great sorrow to find that *some* humans were very small, toothless, unable to speak, unable to walk, and regularly defecated on themselves. But all such anxiety and pity would disappear, according to Spinoza, as soon as they understood that these were called "infants" and that they were perfectly normal and natural in the general chain of development. Knowledge of necessity reduces worry and anxiety. Knowledge that teenage rebellion, for example, is a predictable stage that will eventually pass must give some parents a better ability to weather the storm.

Parental Suffering and Unrealistic Expectations

When Buddhism says "all life is *dukkha*" it means that all life is disappointing or unsatisfactory, but it also recognizes that most of the disappointments and stresses of parenting are caused, not by the child, but by unrealistic expectations in the parents. Sometimes the child is an *extended ego* for the parent – like when I wanted my 5-year-old son to stomp the big kid in his Kung Fu class. Okay, I'm not proud of it, but there it is. Or witness the many cases of the Little League dad screaming at the opposing team, or the neck-tensing, teeth-grinding mother who writhes with worry while her little girl dances in the beauty pageant.

Buddhism reminds us to take a deep breath and try to grasp the natural tendencies and the real personalities of our children. Then try to recognize our own unhealthy expectations, anticipations, demands, and projections. Letting go of our own obsessions regarding our children transforms our disappointments (*dukkha*) into plain old facts. And this realism can help us increase the happiness of our children as well as that of ourselves. Buddhism believes that objective facts can be learned about the attainment of human happiness – facts about psychology, body, and social relations (starting with family). This is not a mystical approach to happiness, but rather a demystified tactic.

The Fourth Perfection, from the *Lotus Sutra*, is *Virya paramita*, which means vigor and effort. An aspect of parenting that gets too little acknowledgment is the fact that it requires tremendous strength – physical and emotional. It *requires* strength, and it *creates* strength. It's not for the frail and the fragile. Buddhism often talks of the strong effort that is required in the disciplining of one's mind, but moral action (e.g., parenting) requires a strong application of emotional and intellectual discipline. The easy and comfortable path of parenting is almost always wrong. Parenting so that your little kid will like you all the time, or wanting your little kid to be your friend and confidant, or wanting your kid to eat whatever she likes, and so on are the roads to perdition – or at least mal-adjusted kids. Hesiod, in *Works and Days*, reminds us that "vice in abundance is easy to get; the road is smooth and begins beside you. But the gods have put sweat between us and virtue." And in the *Anguttara Nikaya* (6.55) the Buddha says that the vigorous person of "right effort" is like the string of a musical instrument. The string cannot be too slack or it won't play (nor can it be too tight, lest it snap). The tension on the string must be continuous and the string must be in tune. So, too, the virtuous person must be ever vigilant. A string that's taut but not overwound is a good analogy for parenting.

The Fifth Perfection of *Dhyana (jhana) paramita* refers to concentration and contemplation. Well, what can I say? Parenting doesn't leave much room for this, at least in the traditional sense of isolated contemplation. Quietly communing with the emptiness of all things is just not on my agenda these days. Thankfully, meditation can also be attained in action, so to speak. Concentration is often characterized as shutting out distraction and focusing on abstract realms of consciousness. But this is only one aspect. The man or woman of action is also supremely concentrated. As a parent, for example, one must be able to shut out distractions – yes, of course, we have to shut out the relentless high-volume shrieking that kids seem to relish so much, but more seriously, we have to shut out the stuff that distracts us from attending to our children properly. Moreover, it takes great concentration to notice the subtle signals and signs that help us promote growth and also reduce peril for our kids.

Wisdom: Family Transcends Religion

Lastly, we have the Sixth Perfection, *Prajna paramita*, which means wisdom. Wisdom is one of those words that can mean almost anything, and anybody with a harebrained idea can dignify her idea with the predicate "wise." But Buddhism means something very specific by wisdom. Buddhist wisdom can be said to be comprised of three big ideas: the wisdom of no-self (*anatta* or *anatman*), the wisdom of impermanence (*anicca* or *anitya*), and the wisdom of dependent arising (*paticca samupadda* or *pratityasamutpada*).

These are the ideas that make Buddhism quite different from its parent philosophy of Hinduism, and also quite different from most Western monotheisms. We already saw, in chapter I, how Hindu metaphysics claims that beneath nature's whirling chaos of *becoming* lies a permanent foundational reality of *being* – called Brahman (or God). In the same way that this permanent reality provides continuity underneath the fluctuations of nature, so, too, an essential eternal soul or self (called *Atman*) provides the continuity underneath each human being. I'm a fluctuating, flowing river of thoughts, emotions, and chemicals, but *Atman* is my true core self – it is the soul that will go on after this life and reincarnate in a new body.

The Buddha rejects this entire picture of reality. The Buddha refutes the ideas of a permanent God and an eternal soul by using three basic strategies: ethical objections, epistemological objections, and metaphysical objections. The last two objections will be discussed more in subsequent chapters, but for now we should contemplate the ethical objections. It has been argued many times, East and West, that the immortality of the soul is a requisite assumption for a moral society. If I am going to perish completely and just be worm-food when I slip this mortal coil, then why not rape, pillage, and burn before I go? The fears and hopes of posthumous justice serve to keep me (and society generally) in line, morally speaking. Fyodor Dostoyevsky famously said, "If God does not exist, then everything is permitted." God and soul go together, on this view, as a kind of *sine qua non* for human morality. The Buddha disagrees, and suggests just the opposite.

Virtue that is based upon the promise of divine rewards and punishments is nothing but *selfishness* extended to a posthumous time-frame. The idea that moral behavior is motivated by a desire to live in Heaven, or rejoin Brahman or

Allah or whatever, is a self-centered view of ethics and one that makes ethics derivative of the desire for self-preservation. The idea that I should be trying to protect my soul and safeguard it into some more pleasurable future life is, according to the Buddha, a cowardly and egocentric approach to ethics. Real compassion, he argues, is better than this egocentrism, and he thinks it flows more naturally from a metaphysical view that gives up the idea of independent, autonomous, souls. We are not separate entities competing to get some pie-in-the-sky. We are threads in a web of living relationships, each one connected to and dependent upon others. Our individuality, especially our supposed eternal individuality, is just a fiction. And it distracts us from seeing the suffering of those around us and prevents us from applying compassion. True compassion does not ask: What do I get out of it?

Is there any evidence that settles the debate? Are believers in immortality more moral than skeptics of immortality? Is it true that a secular or spiritual commitment really makes a big difference in our moral behaviors, our attitudes toward family, work, politics, love, and meaning? While there is an astounding amount of affirmative lip-service to this idea in popular and even high culture, the fact is that true believers and skeptics seem to love their families, pursue fulfilling work, submit to moral duty, and so on, in almost the same way and measure. For every virtuous Christian or Hindu, you can find an evil one, or at least a morally lax one. And the same seems true for atheists. I know many very moral atheists who act compassionately because they feel solidarity with those who are suffering, not because they're going to go to Heaven after death. But if that seems unconvincing, then ask the billions of Confucian Chinese who have lived virtuous lives of family duty (for more than two millennia) without any appeal to an otherworldly God or an immortal soul. You will find that their sense of moral duty stands independently of any metaphysical immortality. Hindus, Muslims, atheists, Buddhists, agnostics, and Christians all love their children (and feel ethically bound to their families). Thankfully, ethics seems to be above and beyond religion.

For the Buddha, giving up the idea of an eternal soul is a part, perhaps the most important part, of giving up the psychology of "me-and-mine." This is why I suggested that parenting is a kind of natural exercise in no-self (*anatta*) philosophy. Perhaps the Buddha was too extreme in his suggestion that Godless, soulless people were *more* ethical and less selfish. But we have to acknowledge that his philosophy made compassion respectable on its own terms, during a time when religion had rendered it as a mere handmaiden to self-interest.

The idea that I have a soul and that my son has one too,

and that no matter what happens to our physical forms we'll be together again forever, is simply too sweet and beautiful for me diminish here. The appeal of this worldview is so obvious that it doesn't even need explanation. Nonetheless, even here the Buddha brings the light of reason. In the *Dhammapada*, he points out that "the fool says: These are *my* sons. This is my wealth. But in reality he is not even the owner of *himself* – how much less of his sons and of his wealth!"

Does this mean that I cannot be attached to my son? Well, if that's what it means, then I wouldn't call myself a Buddhist. No, I think the Buddha is pointing out something that we all understand at some level. He means, rather, that I cannot *possess* my son. Our loved ones are not static objects that we possess and manipulate like curio collections. With regard to children, we parents do the very best we can to create good characters and point them in the right direction, but they grow up and ultimately decide *who* they are and *where* they are going. My son will always be the most important person in my life, but I will also have to let him be himself (especially as he gets older). And down the road, he will have to accept that his very flawed father is neither saint nor fiend – I'm just his Baba.

Obviously, being the member of a family requires a lot of work, sacrifice, deprivation, dedication, and strength. In the United States, where relative wealth exists, the privations are largely distributed over the parents alone. I'm glad of that, and I'm very happy to take any burden I can from my son. But in the developing world, things are different. When I lived in Cambodia and China, I regularly encountered families where the burdens of survival were distributed over the entire family. A child will often do some very difficult labor (e.g., factories, farming, begging, etc.) just to contribute to the survival of the family. Every day I met young boys and girls who were working long hours in order to raise the money to send their brother to school (usually it was a boy, rather than a girl). Most families cannot afford to send every child to school, so they decide on one of them, and then the whole family, including siblings, work hard to pay the tuition for him. He in turn will have tremendous duties and expectations placed upon him when he gets older. He will have to provide for his parents and siblings later in life. The networks of familial support are stronger in the developing countries, in part because they *have* to be. Survival depends upon it.

Overcoming the me-and-mine approach to life, and embracing the no-self approach, is a built-in feature of many family lives – even more so in traditional Buddhist countries and the developing world generally. In the States, we may find that we have to work harder to temper our individual egos. I know many families who do not even talk to each other because of some insult or ancient offense. It is easier, in our prosperous culture, to cut ties and pursue individuality.

"Duty"has almost become a sardonic word in mainstream American society, or at least a word that reeks of hypocrisy. The word lives on with sincerity in many military families, where multiple generations have served honorably. But almost everywhere else, it is treated with suspicion. If insincere politicians are slinging it around casually, it must be nonsense. But a deeper hostility exists for the notion of duty and service. All that American individualism, mixed with Romantic ideas about self-fulfillment and authentic "to thy own self be true" pseudo-philosophy, has produced a people who seem to resent duty.

It might be difficult to see how Buddhism, with its bohemian tendencies, can come to the rescue here. After all Gautama did leave his wife and son to run around the Ganges Valley meditating. His credibility looks a little dubious on this front. To his credit, however, the Buddha did return home eventually and he brought the *dharma* with him. He educated his whole family about the Four Noble Truths, and even converted his business-minded father to the liberating path of no-self.

A Retrograde Social Map?

The Buddha is often interpreted as an other-worldly philosopher, but in fact he gave plenty of temporal advice for people who want to get along better with their spouse, their employer, their parents and children, their friends, and so on. His *Sigalovada Sutta*, or "Code of Lay Ethics," is widely known and followed throughout Southeast Asia and it charts the way that husbands and wives should treat each other, as well as children and parents, employers and workers, teachers and students. The Buddha asks us to envision a social map with the four directional points of East, West, North, and South, but also a third-dimensional axis moving through the middle of the map. The Eastern point represents the relationship of parents and children, the Western point is the relationship between husbands and wives, the North represents friends, the South is teachers and students, the nadir of the central axis represents workers and employers, and the zenith symbolizes spiritual leaders and followers.

The Buddha gives five pieces of advice to each pair of relations. For example, parents should relate to their children by restraining them from doing evil, encouraging them to do good, training them for a profession, arranging a suitable marriage, and leaving them an inheritance. Sons and daughters must relate to their parents by supporting them in old age, fulfilling their duties, keeping the family traditions,

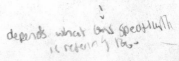

making oneself worthy of an inheritance, and honoring departed relatives. In the Western region of the social map, a husband should respect his wife, be courteous toward her, be faithful to her, hand over domestic authority to her, and provide her with adornment (jewelry, clothes, etc.). In response, a good wife is to perform her duties well, be hospitable to relations, be faithful, protect her husband's earnings, and be skillful and industrious.

I witnessed this domestic division of labor many times when I lived in Asia. By our politically correct standards this map of social relations probably seems retrograde, but let me offer some modest praise for how and why the social system works well in Southeast Asia. I have no interest in suggesting that Americans turn back the clock and live with antiquated social hierarchies, but, in trying to abolish all hierarchies, we have also thrown out the very helpful idea of a division of labor. In my humble opinion, families tend to function better in Southeast Asia, not because there is patriarchy, but, because there is a division of labor. Things would work equally well with a matriarchy or, preferably, with an egalitarian division of labor. But things won't work and don't work when *every* function, task, decision, and authority in a family goes up for debate, competition, rivalry, and opposition. If two people are going to raise a family, then some division of labor is absolutely necessary, and it doesn't matter which gender does which job but it can't be an internal struggle. This was the Buddha's point when he charted the power/responsibility sharing system of the *Sigalovada Sutta*.

Western couples seem constantly locked in a power struggle of no-surrender. Many spouses have a hard time surrendering on any issue because they are constantly in fear of exploitation; they are trapped in opposing postures of self-validation. In a partnership, bowing is not breaking. It is compromise – something we have less and less of in America. Too often, wives feel exploited and husbands feel humiliated. The family dynamic has changed partly because the workforce has changed. But inside many homes (and the divorce rate bears this out) there are significant battles for territory. There are unhappy and unhealthy marriages in Asia, of course, but in Buddhist countries, where one doesn't even believe in a "self," such ego protection seems minimized. The Buddha's lesson of *paticca-samuppada*, or "dependent arising," even applies here in the gender relations (as well as family and work relations). The members of the marriage are not struggling to carve out their own independence, they are interdependent parts of a larger reality. And this reveals the fact that marriage (and family) in the developing world is still an important survival strategy – a strategy that is no longer required in much of the developed world. In the West, *capital* can make family expendable.

The householder (the economic center of the family) is traditionally male in Southeast Asia, but it doesn't have to be. Only the division of labor is necessary, not the gender assignments. And it is necessary primarily so you and your mate can *forget about it*, and get on with the difficulties of raising a family and surviving in a hostile and economically depressed condition. Life is hard enough without warfare and turf disputes inside the sanctuary of your own home.

Americans can't go back in history to some old patriarchy in order to reestablish peaceful harmonic homes and families, nor can they adopt a Southeast Asian way of doing things. But the idea of a family division of labor/power is a flexible, adaptable model. Living with the Buddhist version, and seeing its benefits, made me realize that Americans could do better on the business of family peace. We tend more toward individual fulfillment while Buddhist cultures tend more toward collective flourishing.

The two competing impulses – to be bound to a collective and to be an unfettered loner – are deep in the human psyche. The world religions have always created mythologies and ideals of these life pathways. The monastic impulse toward renunciation is pervasive, but so are the pressing needs of the social animal.

The opposite pull of self-actualization and family duty is handled in traditional Hindu culture by dividing up the lifespan itself. Men in their middle years are expected to be householders – husbands, fathers, breadwinners. However, in later life, once his family obligations are completed, the same man can enter a new life altogether. He can leave behind social ties and turn to ascetic wandering and the cultivation of spiritual wisdom.

There's a nice logic to this system and it seems to work well for some. For one thing, the family and the social ties that are premised on family are protected. And when a man is much older, his desires for bodily pleasure have presumably diminished, so the exploration of unfettered consciousness seems like a more suitable goal. I don't presume to know whether this is the best way to reconcile our two vital tendencies, renunciation and action, but I think Buddhism offers an alternative approach – effective in its own right.

Buddhism suggests that we do not have to compartmentalize our lives, but instead find a *Middle Way* between extremes. I can be a family man of action, instead of a cave-dwelling monk, but I can also elevate my daily actions to a spiritual level by applying mindfulness. Keeping my crazy life in perspective, by remembering *no-self, impermanence*, and *dependent arising*, allows me to be more effective (less overwhelmed) in the chaos of family life.

As a father, I'm frequently frazzled by worry and exhausted from "putting out fires." I have to remind myself that the goal of Buddhism is not liberation from experiences and feelings, but liberation from ego. Ego-consciousness stretches things out of perspective. As a father, I'm never going to become a casual, anything-goes hippy slacker. I can be a frazzled father and still be a good Buddhist. I have to accept this condition. The trick is to not be *overcome* by stress and worry.

All parents I know have had some days, maybe even some months, when they are seriously overwhelmed by the weight of their responsibility and also just depressed and disappointed by something their kids are doing or failing to do. My own parents – bodhisattvas in disguise – must have been tortured by my own troubled teenage rebellion. I had the worst attendance record of anyone in my senior year of high school, and had to be picked up at the police station regularly for minor infractions. I know they suffered, and I'm sure I'll suffer when my son loses his compass and rudder. But hopefully Buddhism will help me to quickly shake off the paralyzing angst, get to the business of analyzing the root causes of the particular drama, and either do something (if it's the sort of thing I can affect) or accept it (if it's not in my power). Of course, there's probably a limit to what Buddhism can do with these raw materials. The *dharma* is strong stuff, but it's not magic and it's not miracle. If your son murders an innocent person, you're probably not going to transcend that suffering and disappointment for a very long time, if ever. Nor can you undo what has been done. Some disappointments are just deeper and more profound than others. It would be obnoxious and fraudulent of me to treat them all optimistically.

Developing Eon Perspective

When you become a parent, you grow some totally new emotions. Like a new limb emerging on your body, complex emotions – previously unfelt – start to twist their way into your mood lexicon. When I reached my 30s I guess I thought I had experienced the full range of human emotions. I had not lived a sheltered life and I had, by then, felt many very strong emotions. But nothing prepared me for the unprecedented emotions of parenthood. Oh sure, there's the obvious stuff, like, you can't believe how much you love this little drooling munchkin. But there's all this other emotional material that emerges as well. For one thing, the guardian feelings of protection and defense became heightened to the stratosphere. I almost drove us off the road once, while trying to keep a mosquito from landing on my baby boy. This and other ridiculous warrior emotions come flooding in. In China, a car came vaguely close to my son's stroller, and I stepped into the street and punched the side mirror clean off the car. The same "near miss" happened a month later in China (which happened a lot, given the overcrowding), and I almost went to jail. These levels of aggression were quite unknown to me before my son was born.

In addition, my longstanding sense of egalitarian fairness was upended by the birth of my son. My liberal dedication to a balanced scale, where every human had equal worth and value, now seemed totally absurd to me. I'd gladly choke a whole room full of people to death, if I thought it would somehow benefit my son. People were not equally worthwhile. There was just my son, and then all the other expendable schlubs in the world. Of course, intellectually I know this is a silly viewpoint, but emotionally I was convinced.

Along with new guardian aggressions, however, came other unfamiliar feelings. The sense of vulnerability is something that everyone feels now and again. But standing with your sick child in the emergency room, while he screams in pain, is an emotion that a nonparent cannot understand. That feeling of vulnerability comes in a magnitude that truly dwarfs everything else. Watching your child suffer, and being unable to fix it is truly the worst feeling that any human being has ever felt. And the anger that it spawns is truly frightening. My point here is that becoming a parent not only brings new responsibilities (that's obvious to anybody), it also brings totally new "ingredients" into your inner life. It creates new and difficult emotional organs.

Buddhism, like Stoicism in the West, seeks to reduce suffering, in part, by managing human emotions. There are several tactics for getting one's emotions under control. One tactic that both Buddhism and Stoicism recommend is the adoption of the long-range perspective. I'll refer to this as *eon perspective*. When we are feeling overwhelmed by anger, or despair, or fear, the Buddha asks us to think about the impermanence of our problems and ourselves. Similarly, Stoic philosopher Marcus Aurelius asks us to contemplate the human drama of families, cities, and even nations that lived hundreds of years ago. They all did just as we do. They married, worked jobs, had children, loved and lost, felt great joys, killed each other, and engaged in every other emotional human endeavor. But, Marcus Aurelius reminds us, "Of all that life, not a trace survives today." It will be no different with the dramas of our own generation.

Of course, eon perspective won't cure every kind of worry regarding family – it will do little, for example, to assuage the anxieties of the emergency room visit. But it might help parents when they're stressing out about what preschool their kid will get into, or SAT scores, or the extra few pounds on the teenager, or the pierced bellybutton, or whatever.

When people asked the Buddha why his followers were

so joyful and healthy when they lived so simply, he replied: "They do not repent the past, nor do they brood over the future. They live in the present. Therefore they are radiant. By brooding over the future and repenting the past, fools dry up like green reeds cut down in the sun." Most of us, of course, are "green reeds cut down in the sun," but we're all searching for a little more of that "radiance."

Chapter IV

Science *Is* Mysticism – without the Magical Thinking

O ne of the reasons why I'm a Buddhist is because Buddhism makes friends of the sciences, and the sciences are the best methods we have for understanding nature. According to a 2009 poll in the *Christian Science Monitor*, Buddhism was the religion most comfortable with evolution theory. When people were asked if evolution was the best explanation for the origins of human life on earth, 81 percent of Buddhists agreed, compared with only 51 percent of mainline Protestants and 45 percent of Muslims. Buddhism is not hostile to biology, psychology, physics, or cosmology. And more than just tolerating each other, Buddhism and science can actually learn from each other.

In the first chapter of this book, I outlined my own youthful mysticism. I was deeply immersed in the arts, and found a powerful camaraderie between the aesthetic life and the spiritual life. I still believe in that camaraderie. But as I got older I became increasingly interested in science. One might say that it was the "aesthetics of science" that first lured me into its deep terrain. Many people, especially critics of scientism, don't even notice that science has its own aesthetic. But when I was a teenager, I became one of the millions of kids who fell under the spell of Carl Sagan's sweeping PBS series *Cosmos* (1980). This thirteen-part television series seems quite dated nowadays, but it is still the most internationally watched series in the history of PBS.

Carl Sagan (1934–1996) introduced my generation to many of the important scientific ideas that shaped the twentieth century. Public school left a lot of gaps in our science education, and Dr. Sagan sought to fill them. What I remember most about the series was not specific theories and facts about planet formation and cell division, but the *romance* of science. State-of-the-art special effects took viewers to the realms of outer galaxies and inner subatomic particles, all the while soaking the audience in a trancelike aural voyage of Vangelis's cosmic soundtrack. Some episodes were downright trippy. All this "edutainment" made for a new kind of science advocacy, and it really worked on me and my generation.

Nature itself is the meeting place for our aesthetic and

scientific interests. Nature is aesthetically beautiful, sublime, and inspirational. But it is also a deep well of microscopic and cosmic causal patterns – facts nested inside facts, all sparking below the surface of appearances. Science unlocks many of those elusive puzzles, and amplifies (rather than reduces) the sense of wonder and inspiration.

Against Magical Thinking

When I was young I felt the lure of Hindu Vedantic philosophy – God is in all things and I am God too (I am *Atman*, and *Atman* is Brahman). And the idea of a secret knowledge (esoteric learning) also fed my elitist tendencies. I'm obviously not alone in this conceit since every religious tradition has some form of gnostic tradition. Belief in a secret cognoscenti – into which you might one day find entry – is the common foundation of widely diverse spiritual yearnings. Think of the Kabbalah movement in Judaism, or the Sufi tradition in Islam, or various conspiracy theories about the Illuminati, or the Five-Percenter movement in the African American Muslim community, or the more recent *The Da Vinci Code* phenomenon (2003), or the New Age variations such as *The Celestine Prophecy* (1993), *The Secret* (2007), and so on.

Most of these worldviews share a common conviction that "positive thinking" and/or secret knowledge can, by itself, rearrange the universe to your liking. *The Celestine Prophecy*, for example, is highly representative of the whole spiritual genre. The book, which has sold over 25 million copies, gives us a hero named John Woodson who goes in search of a secret manuscript that contains nine special insights. Each of these insights brings deeper spiritual understanding of the world and our place in it, and also gets us certain *superpowers* (like flying and turning invisible). Weird coincidences (which should always be interpreted as spiritual "signs") and a hot pursuit by shadowy governmental assassins lead our hero to Peru in search of the manuscript. Our hero attains New Age enlightenment, realizing that there's a mystical force (as in "may the Force be with you") that is guiding all of us to our full blissful actualization.

I believe *The Celestine Prophecy* and other such magical philosophies are popular for one reason: they indulge all our infantile desires to control the world. This is Freud's famous critique of magical thinking, and I find myself in agreement. We all have these infantile desires to control the world through magical means – God only knows what kind of havoc and mayhem I'd wreak if I could fly and turn myself invisible. But I'm not a god or a superhero, and it is juvenile (in the strict Freudian sense) to expect the world to bend to my will. New Age quantum mystics focus on all those innate cravings that healthy socialization has taught us to discipline and repress (so we can live successfully with others), and it reglorifies them in an "adult" philosophy that encourages us to embrace our inner child. My suspicion is that this approach only dresses up narcissism in new garb and calls it "spiritual."

The sciences, thankfully, helped me to grow up and temper my own narcissism. Instead of celebrating prima donna notions of "cosmic consciousness," I came to appreciate my own insignificance. Carl Sagan and the Buddha both helped me to understand that I am but a speck in the universal dust storm. Yes, I'm crucially significant in my little proximate circle of family and friends, but I'm kidding myself if I think that I am the Way and the Truth and Light. This kind of megalomania regularly makes people overly melodramatic about their role in the cosmos – it also frequently leads them to poison the Kool-Aid and foster other delusional tragedies.

Studying biology, physics, cosmology, and the social sciences did not kill my sense of mystery. On the contrary, it made my sense of wonder more pervasive – the mundane became the mystical. I could feel the same sense of wonder by studying the very machinery of nature. I stopped treating the mystical so preciously and began to see it all around me in the mundane. The brain, for example, is probably the most complex piece of equipment in the entire universe, and science has gone through some of its previously closed doors – but every door it goes through opens up on a hundred new ones. Neurobiology, genetics, embryology, evolutionary psychology, and ecology are opening up new and successful ways for us to understand ourselves and our environment. This engagement with the natural world is exhilarating. Studying the Book of Nature can be a spiritual endeavor.

In the same way that Zen Buddhism forced me to retrain my attention on the here and now, rather than on some transcendental realm, science also taught me to sink more deeply into *this* mysterious world. Some people are astonished and exhilarated by stories of astral projection and out-of-body experiences. But I continue to be amazed by the fact that my *thoughts* are somehow moving my fingers on the computer keyboard to type this sentence. I'm equally excited by the fact that my desk seems *solid* to me, when it's really not, and that my spleen, well beneath the radar of my awareness, is quietly destroying redundant red blood cells. How my son's brain, for example, can process English, Chinese, and Spanish is more impressive to me than any miracle of transubstantiation. Or consider the astonishing way that genetic variation and natural selection combine to produce the adaptations of the different human races – a puzzle that called forth only prejudice and bigotry prior to Darwin. Science, for me, just *is* mysticism, clarified and cleansed of its magical narcissistic tendencies.

Much has been made recently of the unique compatibility of science and Buddhism. There is good reason for this connection, and I will try to separate out the strong from the weak ties. First, some quantum nonsense has to be cleared away.

The Dreaded Quantum Mysticism

Many people who have dipped their toes into the waters of Eastern spirituality are wont to rave about parallels between quantum mechanics and Eastern thought. This is a problem. First of all, there is no such thing as "Eastern thought" or "Eastern spirituality." Yes, some similar ideas crop up in Chinese, Japanese, and Indian cultures, but far more dissimilarities exist in their intellectual traditions. Buddhism, for example, is often lumped together with Hinduism, but it should not be. Buddhism is a branch of Hinduism in the same way that Christianity is a branch of Judaism – which is to say, in almost no way. The Buddha rejected many of the major metaphysical ideas in Hinduism, and spent his entire career criticizing Brahminism and Vedantic philosophy. Chinese Confucianism, for example, rejects most Hindu ideas and most Buddhist ideas, while Daoism is almost the mirror opposite of Confucianism. Buddhism itself is disharmonic – Pure Land Japanese Buddhism is almost nothing like Zen Buddhism or Cambodian Theravada. Do they sometimes converge on a specific moral injunction? Yes, of course. But every major religion, East and West, has formulated its own version of the Golden Rule (i.e., do unto others as you would have done to you), and no one is using that as grounds for saying that Presbyterians, Hindus, and Confucians can be lumped together in a meaningful way. So, the idea of an "Eastern spirituality" is largely the invention of sloppy thinking and then marketing people who are trying to sell something.

The purveyors of *quantum mysticism* include Fritjof Capra (the author of *The Tao of Physics*), Deepak Chopra (author of *Quantum Healing*), and the makers of the film *What the Bleep Do We Know!?* (Ramtha's School of Enlightenment). One of the things they are all trying to sell is the idea that there's some deep, ancient agreement on the other side of the planet that we should reject our rationality. And the second major plank in the quantum mysticism campaign is that the conscious mind can and does make reality. Alas, it's not the rational mind, so much as the romantic wanting and willful mind. If you want something badly enough, then your very wanting can actually bend reality to your wish. Why and how would anyone come to this view? And what does it have to do with Buddhism?

There is a very quirky finding in quantum physics, one that suggests an extremely powerful role for the scientific *observer.* It is sometimes called the measurement problem or the observer problem. It all started when Albert Einstein and his generation noticed how light seemed to be a wave under certain experiments and a particle under other experiments. This dual nature – the *wave-particle duality* – unified the previously unconnected domains of particle physics and electromagnetism. This led to the idea that things like light and other subatomic particles could have paradoxically different properties, depending on when and how you looked at them. The description of a thing as a wave includes properties that are contrary to a particle, and vice versa. So how can two mutually exclusive descriptions apply to the same thing?

The paradox is somewhat resolved by the Copenhagen Interpretation, which builds *uncertainty* into the very nature of reality. Electrons, for example, can be reconceptualized as tiny fields or waves – their seemingly determinate singularity is spread out and considered more like a cloud of indeterminate states. But the compromise goes in the other direction, too, because the electron clouds are restricted into small signal centers.

In other words, the indeterminacy is reined into a relatively localizable statistical "point." We can never get precise coordinates on these "things" because as soon as we isolate the position of an electron we always fail to measure its spin or energy. And when we successfully measure its energy, we simultaneously make its position (its coordinated punctiform mass) unintelligible. Determining the position renders the spin indeterminate, and vice versa. This flies in the face of classical Newtonian physics, which suggests that matter has determinate properties or qualities. On the classical model, we may not be able to track all these properties because our science is weak, but at least in principle matter is one way and not another. It's either a wave or a particle, not both. It's either in a specific location or it isn't.

Many, like Einstein, argued that this quantum indeterminacy was just a temporary flaw in our theories and experiments. But the Copenhagen Interpretation said, no, reality itself is actually indeterminate in this way. Uncertainty at this quantum level will not be entirely expunged from our science, because reality itself is only probabilistic rather than determined. This view, not Einstein's, has in fact prevailed in physics. Physicists like Max Born, Werner Heisenberg, and Eugene Wigner noticed that our human level of reality (including causation, space, time, etc.) seemed to operate along classical Newtonian lines, but *below* some boundary line matter took on these more paradoxical quantum qualities. How do all the statistical and indeterminate possibilities of quantum matter become the more determined and recognizable realities of our experience? The Copenhagen solution was to say that the conscious observer actually collapses the potentialities into one actuality, by the very act of observing it. Is it a wave or a particle, is it here or there? The wavefunction collapses into a determinate answer at the moment of conscious experience.

Tremendous confusion surrounds this idea. Mystics have become rapturous in the face of this arcane finding, because they think that it is a corroboration of their romantic world-view. If a conscious observer of quanta actually *causes* wave-function collapse, then, they argue, consciousness can be seen as the true cause of reality. Power of mind over matter, which the spoonbending crowd loves, seems to be confirmed by quantum mechanics. And it's a short jump to Deepak Chopra's "quantum healing" theories about how *erroneous thinking* causes bad physical health in the material body – but *corrected thinking* can actually repair the body. From this cloud of vaguely paralleled and arguable notions – consciousness makes physics, mind presides over matter, even throw in some "action at a distance" for good measure – it's not hard to see that "science" confirms my deep belief that, well, *I make the world.*

First, it has to be said that most of these conclusions are based on (1) debatable interpretations of quantum mechanics and (2) staggeringly fallacious leaps in logic. For one thing, many physicists reject the more philosophical and meta-physical interpretation of the experimental indeterminacy –

preferring an agnostic approach to any metaphysical implications. The data *underdetermines* the paradoxical metaphysics.
Moreover, there appears to be no legitimate extrapolation
from these subatomic findings to our daily human-level
interactions with the world. Quantum uncertainty is a
domain-specific fact of subatomic physics. I do not suggest,
for example, applying a quantum subjective logic to the
question of whether a train is hurtling down the tracks at
your stalled car. We are not walking around town collapsing
wavefunctions as we gaze out at the world.

To underscore the absurdity of applying quantum
mechanics to everyday life, consider Erwin Schrödinger's
famous bizarre thought experiment. Imagine a cat in a box,
with a vial of poison that will be shattered if a connected
Geiger counter detects any radiation. We cannot see inside
the box. According to quantum logic, the cat is both inde-
terminately alive and dead, until we actually look in the box
and collapse the potential reality into an actual reality. The
idea that I make the cat dead or alive by observing it is
manifestly ridiculous and demonstrates the illegitimacy of
applying quantum logic to anything but quanta. At the
human level of reality, Schrodinger's cat is *either* dead or
alive, not both. And when people increasingly talk of
applying quantum mechanics ideas to other domains, like
chemistry, biology, and computing, they are usually referring

to statistical mathematical modeling – they are not making a metaphysical point about an indeterminate reality that is being snapped into determinate shape by conscious observers. In the same way that you cannot *reduce* social science down to chemistry, or people down to genetics, you also cannot extrapolate *up* from electrons to human minds.

I'm tempted to marshal more scientific arguments for why quantum mysticism is misguided, but I'll save time and energy by raising the central, albeit slightly offensive, objection. Quantum mysticism is a juvenile worldview. It starts from a belief that my mind can control matter and destiny, then casts about for any evidence to corroborate that solipsistic view, and finally takes a totally unrelated anomaly of subatomic particles as the aforementioned "evidence."

For most mystics, the mind is an almost miraculous power that lives above and beyond the physical laws. Even for nonmystics like René Descartes and the dualists, the mind is radically separate from the body. According to this view, mind is not determined or constrained in the same way as matter. People who believe that the mind is separate from physical reality tend to locate it as the seat of all *freedom* and personal individuality. Hindu philosophers who see *Atman* as an independent self that goes on after the death of the body, Christians who see the soul (equated with the mind by St. Augustine and St. Aquinas) as detachable from the body,

Cartesians who see the mind as separate from physical laws, and even modern-day New Agers who claim that mind controls physics all agree that mind is a kind of free agent. It may be influenced by the external physical world, but mind is the true actor, decision maker, destiny shaper, manager of the physical realm. The quantum field of collective consciousness supposedly vibrates each of us into existence and when we finally understand that we are luminous beings with power over matter, then we contribute to the critical mass of conscious evolution – eventually, blissful high frequencies will vibrate us to supreme joy. Dream it, and it will happen … . Somebody get me a bucket.

Back Down to Earth: The Buddhist View of Consciousness

Opposed to all this cloying nonsense, we find Buddhism. For the Buddha, the conscious mind is not some miraculous and superior power over matter. It is just one of the causal factors in a matrix of five causes. Unlike all the above dualistic views, which see consciousness as a luminous and possibly immortal power, Buddhism says that consciousness is *always* merged with body, sensation, perception, and volition *(sankhara)*. Consciousness does not ride along in the body for a time, get out when the body dies, and then go on to Heaven, or reincarnate, or merge with Brahman, or even vibrate into the undulating fields of blissful quantum consciousness. Consciousness and other aspects of mind (e.g., volition is both bodily and mental) are always bundled with matter and perception – the *five aggregates* cannot be disentangled in reality.

So for the Buddha, the conscious mind is not above the realm of predictable laws. Rather, it has its own predictable laws. The mind has its own patterns, tendencies, rules, constraints, and potentials. It is complicated and subtle, but it is not some miraculous, magical ghost in the machine. The mind is heavily conditioned (dare I say determined) by discernable laws. The Buddha discovered some of those laws via *introspection*, but there is no reason to think that more recent scientific approaches (more objective than reflective) will negate those introspective discoveries. Brain science, in fact, seems to corroborate some of the Buddha's discoveries about craving and meditation, for example.

For Buddhism and for science, the mind is a natural rather than a supernatural entity. Many people have found this to be a frightening prospect, suggesting that human dignity will be reduced to the dumb clicking of a machine or at best the computations of a digital processor. While there may have been an early tendency toward such reductionism, these days we have a much more nuanced view of the mind and brain. Intellectual decision-making, for example, is saturated with emotions – so much so that people who have the emotive parts of their brains injured cannot even make seemingly simple intellectual choices. Affective systems are intertwined in the intellectual systems. And brains don't really work like machines anyway, but instead reveal hierarchic, recursive, selectional, and adaptive properties. The brain is more like an ecological environment of neurons than a computational digital system. The mind appears to emerge out of this environment of internal brain functions and also the larger environment of the interface between the physiological organism and the external milieu.

Stimuli come into the perceptual equipment, yet the mind/brain is also a projective system – it shapes experiences, formulates representations, and determines meanings. But much of this activity is also happening below the level of conscious awareness, and comprises a subtle dance of impressions, attractions, repulsions, and memories that build up into a personal history. All of these variables combine and produce a person that may be drawn to one kind of pleasure rather than another, and subsequently will evolve specific kinds of obsessions and cravings. Obsession and craving are natural outgrowths of the basic survival equipment of our psychological lives. We're naturally drawn to food, sex, and so on, but we must now take these tendencies into the feedback system of mental reflection and distinguish *extreme* from *moderate* instances of those tendencies.

Science has confirmed that Buddhist meditators have impressive abilities to control unwanted or intrusive thoughts. They also seem to be able to get hold of some otherwise subconscious sympathetic nervous system stuff and shut it off or slow it down or something ... we're not sure. Anybody, however, who doubts the power of Buddhist mental training should read the accounts of Vietnamese monk Thich Quang Duc's self-immolation in 1963. As an act of political protest, he burned himself alive and apparently remained relatively motionless in a lotus position throughout the ordeal.

Unlike many other fans of Buddhism, I am not suggesting that Buddhism has tapped into realms of consciousness that Western science cannot penetrate or account for. On the contrary, I think that Buddhism and science are tandem riders on a naturalistic journey into the mind, and each may learn something from the other. Neurology will help to illuminate what monks have been doing for centuries, and monks may help neurologists avoid the pitfalls of overly reductionistic computational approaches. Even the dominant paradigm of psychotherapy, Albert Ellis's Rational Emotive Behavioral Therapy, shares certain assumptions with Buddhism. Both approaches to psychological healing accept the idea that cognition mediates emotions. This means that redirection of cognitive patterns has the potential to redirect the whole emotive-behavioral complex.

Reflection, habit, and greater understanding of the brain can all help the Buddhist to retrain the mind, or at least slow down the quick jumps from impulse to action. In that sense, Buddhism has always been a science of the mind. But it is not an unrealistic and naive celebration of the mind over *everything* – it is not a mystical subjective idealism.

In the *Shorter Discourse to Saccaka (Majjhima Nikaya, Discourse 35)* the Buddha defends his view that all living beings are comprised of a matrix of five interconnected powers. The great debater Saccaka confronted the Buddha at Vesali, arguing that a core substantial self must underlie all the aggregates. Saccaka argued a familiar Vedantic view – some essential controller (e.g., the Hindu *Atman* or the Christian soul) served the *unity* and the *directionality* of all our various powers (body, perception, etc.). After all, *digestion* doesn't make sense unless we assume the existence of a stomach or some substrate. In the same way that physiological functions seem to require a substratum, isn't it also true that the different functions and powers of man require a soul or self to serve as foundation? And isn't this the true conscious self, the controller of our destiny and the maker of our *karma*? The Buddha says, no.

The Buddha recognizes that Saccaka is looking for an identifiable *agent* in the matrix. Mystics and dualists settle on one member of the federation – usually conscious mind – and elevate that member to the status of controller. Saccaka thinks of the *essential self* as a kind of king, a monarch who has power and control over his subjects. The quantum mystics have a similar view of conscious mind – it is the director of all things. But despite the emotionally comforting aspect of this belief (i.e., I'm in control), the Buddha wants to know if there's any evidence for this belief. If the conscious mind has ultimate control over the *khandas*, the Buddha says, then I should be able to wish my *body* into any shape or size that I want. So, too, I should be able to wish my *sensations* to be whatever I want, and my *perceptions* to be whatever I want. Do you, the Buddha asks Saccaka, have this kind of limitless power over your body and perceptions? And Saccaka has to admit that he does not. The Buddha claims that there is no *evidence* for a controller self, only the *desire* to be one. Once we give up on this exaggerated delusion of control, we attain some degree of liberation – we stop trying to *own* everything; this is *my* experience, this is *mine*, this is *I*, this is *myself*.

Every aspect of ourselves (all the *khandas*) are impermanent, and they seem to take turns controlling or dominating our experience. The mind does have considerable power, and that power can be increased by mental cultivation, but it is not capable of erasing the other causal powers. Nor can the mind, or some other soul entity, constitute an eternal piece of pure reality. In the *Nandakovada Sutta*, the Buddhist monk Nandaka argues that it is silly to keep insisting on a permanent mind or soul within us. He draws a *reductio ad absurdum* analogy for his audience of nuns. "When a lamp is burning, its oil is impermanent and liable to change, and so are its wick and its flame," so it is irrational to believe that "its *radiance* is permanent, everlasting, eternal, and not liable to change." If our perception, body, sensation, volition, and consciousness are all impermanent, then how can we legitimately invent some mysterious permanent force that rides parallel to these and then outstrips them into the future? Rather, the self is an epiphenomenon that emerges as a consequence of the conditioned causal matrix. If there is a felt sense of a self, and surely there is, then it is metaphysically like the shadow of a tree. If you remove the impermanent tree, there is no leftover shadow.

But wait, you might protest. There is something odd about *consciousness*, in the sense that it seems less tangible and more separate from the other bodily *khandas*. Perhaps it is a good candidate for a privileged place in the human package – perhaps it controls things and also goes on after bodily death. But in *Discourse 38* of the *Majjhima Nikaya*, the Buddha points out that every moment of consciousness that we have ever experienced has always been mixed or dependent upon its sensual or ideational condition. Consciousness is bound by the same relation of dependent arising that binds everything else. Consciousness has no special independence. We have ear consciousness, eye consciousness, nose consciousness, tongue consciousness, skin consciousness, and mind consciousness, but no pure, unmixed, separable consciousness. He says that every fire is produced by its particular conditions – there are log fires, grass fires, cow dung fires, and so on. But there is no pure fire independent of material conditions. The same is true of consciousness. When consciousness is aware of the hand grasping an item, then it is in a dependent relation with the body and perception. But if it is aware of a concept (e.g., a number), then it is dependent upon the abstracted symbol that mental manipulation creates out of the raw stuff of impressions. There is nothing supernatural in any of this.

Why, then, is there so much common misperception about Buddhism, quantum mysticism, and cosmic mind? The answer is straightforward, albeit maddening because the confusion leads to an erroneous view of Buddhism. Like any tradition, Buddhism has evolved, fractured, reformed, waxed, waned, devolved, and corrupted. It has split many times on doctrinal and political grounds, the most well known being the Mahayana and Hinayana split. This is a rather tired and unilluminating distinction, so I won't spend too much time on it. There are many things that define the differences between Hinayana (the smaller path) and Mahayana (the larger path), including historical dominance and just geographical distribution (e.g., Hinayana lives on in the Theravada Buddhism in Southeast Asia, while later Mahayana – including Zen, Pure Land, Tantric, etc. – developed more in the Far East). Mahayana also stresses the importance of bodhisattvas (Buddhist saints) more than does the earlier Hinayana tradition. But I will bracket all the disagreements of the major Buddhist schism, and focus instead on the metaphysical disputes that emerged.

As Buddhism evolved in the centuries after Gautama's death, it elaborated the metaphysical theories of the early teachings. A whole body of scriptural texts known as *Abhidhamma* (special *dharma*) emerged, together with later sutras known collectively as the *Prajnaparamita Sutras* (including the *Heart* and *Diamond sutras*). These texts entered into new metaphysical territory. They began to talk of *dhamma* (Pali) or *dharma* (Sanskrit) in a new way. Yes, it still meant the teachings of Gautama, but it also became the term used to describe the atomic unit or element of reality.

Remember that Gautama criticized the idea of independently existing entities, and argued that all things are interconnected and dependent on other things. Nothing is self-subsistent, nothing has a fixed essence. Everything is what it is in *relation* to other things. Humans, for example, who think they are independent essential souls, have made this essentialist error in thinking. Gautama analyzed humans and other living beings down to their compositional parts/powers, the five *khandas* – and he eliminated the soul in the process. But later Buddhist philosophers began to further dissect the five *khandas*. At first,philosophers of the Abhidhamma began to break down experience into smaller element units, called *dhammas*. A sensation *dhamma* of red, for example, and a sensation *dhamma* of round, and a sense *dhamma* of sweet, and so on all converge to form the higher-level experience of eating an apple. This approach tried to lay out the building blocks of our daily experience – tried to create a taxonomic classification of experiential occasions. But then a more metaphysical tone arose in the discussions of the *Prajnaparamita Sutras* (and their competing interpreters, like Nagarjuna's Madhyamaka school and the Yogacara school).

In the same way that Gautama had dissected a person into five *khandas*, the Abhidhamma tradition dissected *khanda* experience further into elemental atoms *(dhammas)*. And now, the Mahayana philosophers (like those in the Madhyamaka and Yogacara schools) began to argue about the metaphysical status of these atoms. Were the atoms real and self-subsistent, like Democritus's atomic building blocks, or were they empty of being, impermanent, and dependent like everything else? One group (the Madhyamaka) took the position that the atoms were empty – that is to say, impermanent just like everything else. The Yogacara seem to have maintained that the atoms were real in some way (i.e., essential, self-subsisting, and quasi-permanent). But as if that wasn't complicated enough, it gets worse. The Yogacara philosophy came to be known as the Consciousness-Only school. It's hard to reconstruct all this, but it appears that since every human experience always refers back to consciousness, then the mind is the only thing that we can truly say to exist. Even an experience of a body, like a felt pain in my foot, is ultimately only available to me via the subjectivity of consciousness. So subjective mind is the only thing we have real contact with, and therefore it made sense to the Consciousness-Only school to say that it is the only reality. Mind, which is made up of consciousness atoms or seeds, is the condition of all of reality.

So, this is where the quantum mystics are getting their Buddhism from – a highly idiosyncratic offshoot of Mahayana (the Consciousness-Only school), which had confusing impact on subsequent Chinese and Tibetan Buddhism, and which constitutes a corruption of all early Buddhism. The famous Chinese monk Xuan Zang, for example, brought these ideas back from India, but they did not really catch on and they seem to have mutated further (surviving in strains of Tibetan Buddhism). Some scholars have said that the teachings represent a true subjective idealism and a true precursor to the New Age idea that mind makes or controls the physical world. Others interpret the Consciousness-Only school as simply focusing on and isolating the causes of bad *karma* (i.e., only conscious decisions create *karma*), and that they were largely unconcerned with other metaphysical debates. Whatever the case, it is clear that New Age versions of Buddhism are based upon idiosyncratic later permutations, not on the original or mainstream teachings.

No Giordano Brunos or Galileos Here

The true reason for a Buddhism/science interface is not some agreement on quantum subjectivity. Instead, Buddhism and science share a similar approach to phenomena, an approach that can be called *naturalism*. Naturalism rejects (or at least brackets) supernatural explanations of the world and its occupants (e.g., us). Unlike many other religions, Buddhism does not find itself in the awkward position of having to reconcile the metaphysical assertions of faith with the experimental findings of science. There have been no egregious Buddhist persecutions of scientists – no counterparts to Giordano Bruno and Galileo. Nor have there been the embarrassing and tortuous attempts of creation science to twist every scientific finding into the shape of a biblical prognostication. Buddhism is not trying to remake all knowledge into the image of its own scriptural visage.

There are two major reasons why Buddhism reconciles so smoothly with science. First, it is officially agnostic (and practically atheistic) when it comes to God and the soul. Second, it is not a tradition of revelation, but an experimental approach to knowledge and truth. Metaphysical obsessions about the origin and purpose of the universe – which are fundamental to Western faiths – are off the docket in Buddhism. The Buddha thinks that questions about the infinity of the universe or the immortality of the soul are effectively impossible to answer, and they tend to distract the searcher from the present moment and the overcoming of suffering. He calls these "*avyakata* questions," or unanswerable questions. In the *Cula-Malunkyovada Sutta (Majjhima Nikaya* 63), the Buddha says:

> Should anyone say that he does not wish to lead the righteous life under the Enlightened One, unless the Enlightened One first tells him whether the world is eternal or temporal, finite or infinite; whether the life principle is identical with the body, or sometimes different; whether the Perfect One continues after

death, etc., – Such a person would die, before the Perfect One could tell him all this. It is as if a man were pierced by a poison arrow, and his friends, companions, or near relations called in a surgeon but that man should say: I will not have this arrow pulled out until I know who the man is that has wounded me; whether he is a noble, a prince, a citizen, or a servant; or whether he is tall or short, or of medium height. Truly such a man would die, before he could adequately learn all this.

In place of speculative adventures of the imagination, the Buddha puts pragmatic empiricism. The Four Noble Truths, for example, should be considered as testable hypotheses. Their truth or validity can be ascertained by anyone willing to run the experiments. Does detaching from craving actually reduce one's suffering? Don't take the Buddha's word for it.

The Buddha goes so far in the direction of pragmatic empiricism that he even warns us to avoid dogmatizing Buddhism. The *dharma* is a raft, he explains. It should be used to get over troubled waters. Imagine if a man used a raft to get over a raging river, but once he was safely on the other side he said to himself: "This raft is so helpful that I'm going to strap it on my back and carry it around with me for the rest of my life." No less absurd is the person who clings irrationally to his religion, even when its usefulness is over.

If the Buddha could find no evidence for a claim, he generally set it aside and took an agnostic or even critical attitude. He could find no evidence that animal sacrifices worked to influence the future or to atone for misdeeds, so he discarded the practice and the belief. Same thing when it came to the existence of a cosmological caste system, or the existence of an unseen eternal soul.

While there is no legitimate quantum mysticism–Buddhism synthesis, we might note a few more modest metaphysical parallels. Since Buddhism criticizes anything absolute, eternal, and perfect, we might say that it fits nicely with the *probability* paradigm in contemporary science. In physics, chemistry, biology, and the social sciences, we have progressed in the twenty-first century to a probabilistic model of knowledge rather than a search for absolute indubitable certainty. The old quest for certainty has been seen to be a pipedream, but science proceeds just fine – even thrives – without such incontestable foundations. The statistical approach to science fits nicely with a Buddhist conviction that everything is changing, everything has exceptions, and everything is contingent on other things. And along these same lines, we might draw a modest parallel to the Darwinian revolution, which also rejected fixed essences. Darwin overthrew a long tradition of typological thinking that said that nature had eternal forms (e.g., species) incarnate in matter. Darwin showed that even these seemingly fixed and eternal forms were also undergoing slow transmutation. There is no permanent ideal great-chain-of-being behind the fluctuating appearances of nature. There's just nature.

This is not to say that evolution proves Buddhism or Buddhism proves evolution. Such an agenda strikes me as childish. Let them prove themselves, if they can. If they're warranted or justifiable, then they will demonstrate it. The one endeavor does not sink or swim with the other. I only wish to point out why Buddhism can integrate so well with the sciences.

Robots Need Enlightenment Too

Everyone knows the story of Galileo and also the creation science versus evolution debate, but Western religions have also been tremendously uneasy about *technology*. Ever since Mary Shelley gave us the Frankenstein monster, we have been employing it as a cautionary metaphor for every technological advance. In 2008, for example, a survey found that religious countries were much more opposed to nanotechnology than secular countries. In the survey, published in *Nature Nanotechnology*, the United States was found to be the most religious country and also the most hostile and wary of nanotechnology.

Western religion, with its idea of a creator God, permeates our culture and sanctifies life in such a way that any technological manipulation of life seems arrogant and offensive. Buddhism, on the contrary, has no belief in a creator God and therefore feels none of the anxiety about scientists using technology to "play God." There might be very good reasons not to pursue certain technological moves, like cloning and other biotechnology, but for Buddhists those reasons will appeal to the dangerous and unforeseen consequences. Buddhists do not rule out certain kinds of technology on the grounds that life is sacred and God will be angered by our hubris. Actually, I should refine this further. Life *is* sacred for Buddhists – all life, not just human life. But it is not sacred because a deity breathed life into it. Rather, any living thing is comprised of the five *khandas* and therefore susceptible to pain and suffering. It is everyone's duty, then, to understand their connection to all life and to employ compassionate action for the alleviation of suffering.

In Western religions, however, there is usually a yawning chasm that separates we humans from the nonhuman creatures. We are made in God's image. They are not. There is something *miraculous* about life, and something even more miraculous about we humans. Buddhism does not share this species elitism, nor do Buddhists believe that life can only happen miraculously. We were not made better than everything else by a loving God at the beginning of creation. Rather, all living beings, according to Buddhism, are trying to make themselves better by their own powers and abilities. We are all trying to work out our enlightenment and liberation.

There are gods and spirits in the cultures of Buddhism, but they are more like superheroes or supervillains. They are not omnipotent, omniscient, or omnibenevolent. And these other intelligent beings (devas, ghosts, animistic spirits, etc.) are, like us, trying to work out their own enlightenment. They might be more powerful or live longer than us, but that does not mean that they are free or awakened.

So, for Buddhism, *life* is defined more by function – by physiology rather than by religious metaphysics. If, in our near future, technology produces smart robots, and clones, and nano-beings, and artificial intelligence, and even artificial life, then Buddhism will simply offer its usual advice: let's help these new beings also as they pursue their enlightenment with diligence.

The Science of *Karma* and Rebirth?

Now it's only fair to point out some radical disagreements between Buddhism and science. Buddhism tends to stay close to human experience (e.g., suffering, craving, liberation, etc.), and it asks people to try its teachings like one might try any other experiment. But two glaring exceptions to this empirical approach can be found in the doctrines of *karma* and *rebirth*.

Karma literally means "action," but usually means the law of action that rewards good deeds with good consequences (the fruits of *karma*) and bad deeds with bad consequences. Rebirth (*samsara*) means "to come again and again" and Westerners usually refer to it as reincarnation. Both these ideas are caught up in Buddhism and Gautama used them frequently in his lectures, but they are much older ideas and date back to Vedic and Upanishad Hinduism. In Hinduism these ideas actually make more sense because Hindus subscribe to the idea of an eternal soul (*Atman*) that goes from one life to the next, creating and receiving karmic rewards and punishments. Buddhism on the other hand has eliminated the transmigrating soul, but still preserved the doctrines of *karma* and rebirth.

Many Western and Eastern apologists for Buddhism will do conceptual backflips to defend the reasonableness of *karma* and *samsara*. I see no reason to join them. There is no good evidence that *karma*, for example, is real. In fact there seems to be quite good evidence to the contrary – bad people flourish all the time and good people suffer terribly. The idea that there a cosmic force that functions like a law of nature and ensures that everybody eventually gets what they deserve seems much more like wishful thinking than fact. I wish *karma* were true. But I also wish I could fly and make myself invisible.

Of course, any theory of posthumous justice – like *karma* or the Christian Heaven and Hell – has certain benefits for the development of human social harmony. And we can assume that this more pragmatic consideration illuminates the tenacity of such dubious ideas through history. When I lived in Asia, for example, I observed that the pursuit of good *karma* and upwardly mobile rebirth is a daily concern for cultural Buddhists. And some Westerners too have been very attracted to *karma* and *samsara* as a consoling alternative to the usual stories of pearlygates and lakes of fire. But the only really compelling interpretation of *karma* – one that doesn't conflict with science – is the radical reinterpretation that asks us to think about *karma* as a psychological fact rather than a metaphysical one. For example, it is possible to say that one's *early* lack of mental control and discipline results in a *later* batch of suffering – perhaps I never disciplined my cravings for fast food as a young man, and now I'm an obese older man who lives like a slave to Frenchfries. Or my *younger* taste for drama and negative attention has resulted in a *later* relationship pattern wherein I only try to date married women. This more naturalized version of *karma* is the only one that seems reasonably defensible.

Rebirth is an equally problematic doctrine. For Hindus, reincarnation of *Atman* over and over again is an idea that at least has conceptual coherence, but (like *karma*) it also fails dreadfully at the court of experience. Some New Age believers will no doubt object and bleat on about how they remember their past lives, but the fact that such credulous folks always remember themselves as famous historical persons is probably enough to eliminate such "evidence"from the bank of legitimate data. Moreover, even the official Hindu doctrine of *Atman* locates conscious memories in the ego and body, and these are left behind during the transmigration – only the pure *Atman* carries on.

Buddhism has a more obscure doctrine of rebirth. The soul does not go on after death,because there is no soul in Buddhism.So what is getting reborn? This was a common mystery even during the Buddha's lifetime and in the subsequent centuries of Buddhist philosophy. Instead of thinking of a permanent substance or ghost continuing on, the Buddha says we should understand that the five aggregates (the *khandas*) continue on. Body, sensation, perception, volition, and consciousness are like flowing streams of energy. They coalesce for a time and make up persons, but they also keep flowing when those persons cease. It is like our contemporary scientific idea of the conservation of matter – matter/energy gets rearranged but it does not disappear during these transformations. The Buddha's commitment to a kind of natural causality means

that *later* events are heavily (some might say deterministi-
cally) influenced by the paths of *earlier* ones. In this way,
Buddha believes that *karma* can hold across lifetimes.
Perhaps the most famous analogy to make sense of this
flowing rebirth model is the flame simile. When challenged
on the coherence of his doctrine, the Buddha and
subsequent philosophers have described a candle or a lamp.
Imagine that we light the candle and it burns for a time.
Now we use the candle to light a second candle and blow
out the first. After a time we do the same with a third,
fourth, and fifth candle. It does not make sense, the
Buddha suggests, to ask whether it is the *same* flame at
candle five as it was at candle one. It is not even the same
flame as it burns on the first candle, because it is a
dependent convergence of combustion processes. So, too,
rebirth of living beings is not a movement of a self-same
soul, but a causal process that links earlier and later
(temporary) unities.

This is relatively sophisticated philosophy. It reorients us
from thinking about substances to processes or functions. But
anyone can see that it is also deeply unsatisfying to our
emotional desires for immortality. Yes, energy will go on and
on, but *I* won't be there to experience it. Despite the warm
and fuzzy way that such rebirth is discussed in New Age
literature, there is in fact nothing very consoling about the

idea that I and my loved ones will die, disintegrate, and get rearranged into other stuff. Of course, for Buddhism, that's the point. The Buddha is not interested in stroking our egos, comforting us, or feeding our emotional cravings.

Despite the cold-bath reality-check of the Buddha's doctrine of rebirth, it is a lamentable but understandable fact that many later Buddhists fell back into a more Hindu notion of reincarnation. Even the Dalai Lama, for example, will talk today about reincarnations, when such ideas bear little resemblance to the actual philosophy of historical Buddhism. But even the more scientifically respectable idea that rebirth just means the conservation of matter is not very interesting or significant. It might be true, but it seems trivially true, upon reflection – especially when we remember that overcoming suffering is the major goal of Buddhism.

Here is my somewhat radical suggestion. There is nothing particularly Buddhist about either of these meta-physical doctrines – *karma* and rebirth. Yes, we hear Buddhists regularly intone such doctrines, but do they have any necessary connection to the Four Noble Truths? My contention is that they do not. They are leftovers from pre-Buddhist religion and found their way onto the Buddhist plate for cultural, not philosophical, reasons. The perennial popularity of such doctrines (which lack empirical validity) is attributable to the deep emotional desires in all human beings – some of which are beautiful, like the desire to see my dead relatives again.

Each Buddhist has to decide for herself which aspects of the *dharma* seem reasonable. People can hold on to *karma* and rebirth if they want to – it's a free country. But let's not confuse the scientifically compatible aspects of Buddhism with the incompatible aspects. I have seen fans of Buddhism try desperately to build a scientific basis for the speculative wishful thinking of *karma* and reincarnation. But, for me, recognizing that suffering comes from craving and craving can be trained away has no logical dependence on the idea that people get what they deserve (*karma*) or the idea that we'll all get to live again after death (rebirth). Applying Ockham's razor to our beliefs is something the Buddha would have approved.

I am a Buddhist, in part, because it does not require me to sacrifice my critical thinking skills. Martin Luther famously exhorted believers that, if they wanted to be good Christians, they should "tear the eyes out of their Reason." Buddhism does not ask us to negate our personal rationality or our scientific rationality. It does not ask us to accept things on faith alone. That is not to say that faith is useless or silly. But it does mean that we cannot divinize our own wishful thinking into bogus cosmic principles, and then pretend like we've discovered them in the firmament of transcendental truth.

Chapter V

Jack Kerouac, Haiku, Charlie Parker, and the Artistic Quest

The relationship between art and the *dharma* is an important reason why I am a Buddhist. Since I'm not a believer in the Abrahamic God, or the immortal soul, or an eternal afterlife (the stuff of Western religions), I tend to stress the role of art as the main vehicle of transcendence. Religion has always played a major role in lifting people out of the selfish concerns of their little egos, but good art does the same thing and spares us the speculative metaphysics and leaps of faith. Standing before a beautiful painting, hearing a sublime piece of music, or losing oneself in a powerful drama are not merely experiences that are similar to meditation, they *are* meditations. Buddhism and art are partners in the pursuit of illumination and inspiration.

Appreciating art and making art are meditations that

liberate us from self-absorption. The Greeks recognized this decentering of the ego and talked about artists as inspired (literally taken over) by the Muses. We still talk this way. After the great Texas blues guitarist Stevie Ray Vaughan died, Eric Clapton paid tribute by describing him as "an open channel ... music just flowed through him." When I worked as a blues musician in Chicago, playing with greats like Buddy Guy, Bo Diddley, and B. B. King, I saw this "channeling" firsthand. It didn't happen all the time or even most of the time, but when it did it was something special. Since I obviously don't believe in the actual "channeling of spirits" I naturally think something else is going on – something that we describe with the metaphor of spirit "possession." What's going on in an artistic spell is, I believe, the same as in a Buddhist mindful meditation. In what follows, I will explore the many ways that art and Buddhism converge in this pursuit of transcendence.

As a religious culture, Buddhism has had all the mythological drama that other religions artistically portray – demons, saints, miracles, adventures, and the like – but it has something else too. It has a spiritual interpretation of the aesthetic experience itself. It is not just interested in art as a representation of religious stories. Generally speaking, Buddhism is not *morally* interested in art. Buddhism almost abstracts the moral and theological *content* out of these works and focuses more on the formal elements and the unique psychology they produce.

I think the role of art is especially important in Buddhism, because Buddhism embraces a nondualistic metaphysics. In some *supernatural* religious frameworks art is a gateway or communication to a divine realm, but in Buddhism the artistic experience is "naturalized" like everything else. This is why Buddhists have always been more interested in the psychology of art. Art is a meditation that brings one in contact with the formless nondiscursive mind. So, it's not a mere *communication* with a transcendent reality, it *is* a transcendent reality. As an analogy, I think "memory" becomes more important in the secular Confucian framework of the Chinese, because there is no supernatural immortality – only an "afterlife" in the memories of your descendents.

Emptiness between the Brush Strokes

When I was an undergraduate student, I studied painting before I switched my major to philosophy.(My parents should be congratulated for enduring my utter lack of pragmatic direction.) Amid my peripatetic explorations of art history, I became obsessed with Japanese and Chinese calligraphy (and also the abstract expressionism of American painter Franz Kline – whose paintings look like "close-ups" of Asian calligraphy). I'm not entirely sure, to this day, why this stuff speaks to me, except to say that these works tend to point at themselves rather than out at the world. They're not representational paintings of people, or dogs, or mountains, or crucifixions. Since I couldn't read Japanese or Chinese when I was an undergraduate, it became obvious that it was the lines, strokes, brush marks, and negative spaces themselves that appealed to me. Even among native readers of Chinese *hanzi*, calligraphy is a high art form because of its own inherent style and formal beauty, not just because the poems or semantic sentiments are noble. Lines on paper, which do not necessarily represent or point to anything else, have a kind of elegant clarity that parallels the purified empty mind of Buddhism.

It's interesting to think about artworks and genres in relation to their unique metaphysical contexts. The scroll paintings of China, Korea, and Japan tend to employ huge swaths of unapologetic negative space. A mountaintop hut peeking out from a vast stretch of white fog and cloud. Rivers, dragons, and cherry blossom trees only suggested and glimpsed from behind swirling mists. Whether it's calligraphy, landscape paintings, or haiku poems, the Far East has always celebrated the "less is more" aesthetic. By contrast, Indian art, and the Indianized cultures of Southeast Asia, celebrate the "more is more" philosophy and cram characters, colors, and writhing forms onto every paintable surface. Indian metaphysics is largely concerned with the idea of an unmanifest being (Brahman) expressing or manifesting its infinitely fecund power in myriad physical forms. Complexity, intricacy, and sheer density of imagery are respectful and fitting communications of God's awesome power. *Mandalas*, for example, are wonderful examples of the Indian idea (in both Hinduism and Buddhism) that the macrocosm can be found inside the microcosm. To paraphrase Gottfried Leibniz, "every single substance is a perpetual living mirror of the universe." And in Tibetan Buddhism the *mandalas* also convey the Buddhist teaching of impermanence (*anicca*), because when the elaborate and agonizing sand-paintings are finally finished, they are immediately and intentionally swept away and destroyed.

The Far Eastern traditions of Daoism and Zen Buddhism, on the other hand, have turned away from the spiraling complexity of forms. Negative space and the aesthetics of minimalism help to convey the equally powerful *emptiness* between things. It's the often forgotten empty space, or the vacant shape in the middle of a bowl or a cup, which makes it useful, or valuable. Without this vacant emptiness, a bowl will not even be a bowl. This is a very Chinese approach, and it conveys the importance of the yin-yang relationship of something and nothing, being and nonbeing, action and nonaction. *Wu-wei* is a Chinese word that is often translated as "nonaction" but more accurately means "natural action" or action in accordance with nature. The idea, dominant in Daoism and Zen, is that one should try to find the natural way of doing something and then conform or align oneself to it, as opposed to forcing a human conventional effort onto some process. For example, the butcher should carve the animal at its joints, not in arbitrary locations. A sculptor should work *with* the grain of wood, rather than against it. A martial arts master should find the most economic use of his energy, and turn his opponent's own force to his advantage. A calligraphy stroke should follow the natural smooth movements of the wrist and forearm, and so on. Finding this natural way is not effortless, but requires great work. Once it has been mastered, however, then one finds a unique presence of mind in these activities. The actions are turned into artistic expressions.

The "less is more" aesthetic of the Far East helps to convey some Buddhist ideas about the emptiness of forms (the unreality of essential substances), but the artwork also engenders in the viewer the kind of mental composure that *nirvana* aims toward. Chinese landscape paintings, for example, are very good at assuaging and harmonizing the troubled and scattershot mind. Or consider the minimalist beauty of Yosa Buson's Japanese haiku:

At a roadside shrine,
before the stony Buddha
a firefly burns

Life Itself Is an Artwork

The activity of the artistic *process* itself is celebrated as a gateway to mindful awareness – awareness of the present moment. Is it any wonder that many Western artists, and art lovers, have been drawn to Buddhism? But since Buddhism is a *method* or skill, as much as a doctrine, then it can be practiced in every aspect of life.

Zen Buddhism in particular has the unique ability to transcend its historical and cultural context, giving new shape and direction to searchers of every creed. It does this by steering clear of dogma, focusing instead on the *method* of your life rather than the content of your life. Zen fits well with Western ideas of personal authenticity. It's not so much *who* you are or even *what* you do in life. Rather, it's *how* you do it. Since the present moment is ultimate reality (albeit usually obscured and hidden in regular consciousness),all one need do is shut off the babble of discursive thought and sink into one's present activity. According to this view, the *meaning* of life is not found in theology or even morality. Almost like Western existentialism, Zen is skeptical about rules, formulas, commandments, categorical imperatives, and cultural norms.

After the "death of God," Friedrich Nietzsche (and the subsequent existential philosophers) did not give in to nihilism or even pessimism. In *The Gay Science*, Nietzsche says: "*One thing is needful* – To 'give style' to one's character – a great and rare art! It is practiced by those who survey all the strengths and weaknesses of their nature and then fit them into an artistic plan until every one of them appears as art and reason and even weaknesses delight the eye." Here we have a Western version of the Zen insight that one's whole life can be a kind of artwork. Attending carefully to one's actions and choices – *owning* them, so to speak – brings authenticity to life. Rather than a theological or moral approach, it is an aesthetic approach to meaning.

Buddha Wears a Beret: American Artists Discover the *Dharma*

One of the most intense American flirtations with Buddhism is probably the Beat movement of the 1950s and 1960s. As I mentioned earlier, the Beats had a big influence on my early Buddhism (I even bought a beret and everything), even though I was born around the time that the movement was dying – or rather, around the time it was *transforming* into other expressions of counterculture. The Beats and their descendents are worth further exploration because their relationship with the *dharma* highlights many of the more universal *artistic interests* in Buddhism.

Jack Kerouac's influential *The Dharma Bums* (1958) attempts to be a Zen-like story of unexpected, spontaneous, almost accidental grace. It tries to erase the high/low line and unite the sacred and profane – the spiritual and the absurd. But to press the absurdity of Zen even more, and take it farther afield of its hushed and sacred milieu, we have to at least mention *The Beverly Hillbillies* episode where Jethro becomes a beatnik and Granny has to rescue him. While in the beatnik coffee shop, Granny accidentally invents the hip new beatnik dance called the "shovelin' taters." The episode is a little known 1965 Zen masterpiece, and includes Jethro's great line, "Aww Granny, you just blew my gig! Now I ain't beat!"

And one last Zen gesture, to suck the air out of the room by reference to Jed Clampett and company; I have to at least mention that Kerouac himself was a fan of *The Beverly Hillbillies* and could scarcely break away from it in 1966, when his estranged pregnant daughter came to visit him. He had only met his daughter one time before, after a paternity test finally forced him to acknowledge her. That previous meeting, when Jan was only 9 years old, consisted partly in Kerouac taking her to a liquor store. The young girl saved the cork from the Harvey's Bristol Cream sherry in order to remind herself that she really did have a father. At their second meeting, Kerouac reportedly turned away from the TV just long enough to arrogantly instruct the struggling Jan to "write a book … you can use my name."

This episode doesn't exactly conjure up the Buddha's "heart of compassion." When I learned about it recently, I began to wonder about the precise role of Buddhism in Kerouac's life. Of course, charging a writer with hypocrisy by throwing his own foibles in his face is a low blow. But what was it in Buddhism that attracted this whole generation of hipsters (and, for that manner, subsequent generations of hipsters)?

Beat poet Gary Snyder, who serves as the main character in Kerouac's *The Dharma Bums*, tried more recently to capture the unifying and animating spirit of the Beat movement. "It's very interesting," Snyder reflects, "that we find ourselves so much on the same ground again, after having explored divergent paths; and find ourselves united on this position of powerful environmental concern, critique of the future of the individual state, and an essentially shared poetics, and only half-stated but in the background very powerfully there, a basic agreement on some Buddhist type psychological views of human nature and human possibilities."

One of the attractions of Buddhism is that it points out the *conventional* nature of many "truths" that we think of as natural facts. Bohemian artists, who dislike rigid and fixed societal expectations, are drawn to the idea that the everyday routine world is illusory. As we've already discussed, in Buddhism there are levels of reality. The top level is pretty much the world we see around us. Our day-to-day experiential world is made up of individual beings who seem separate or individuated from each other. There's a guy named Steve Asma, and there's a guy named Allen Ginsberg, and there's a woman named Rosa Parks, and there's a guy named Ted Bundy, and there's a dog barking outside my window, and so forth. And these beings are relatively the same with themselves (over time), but different from each other. However, if you go down beneath this conventional layer of reality, you find a deeper layer in which each being is only a momentary confluence of five streams or aggregates (*khandas*), namely, body, sensation, perception, will, and consciousness. The idea of compositional levels here is not much different from what we already accept from the physical sciences, just not as reductionist. We are accustomed, for example, to seeing that biological organisms are composed of smaller and less visible chemical interactions, while those chemical interactions are themselves composed of atomic and subatomic physics interactions. And, in Buddhism, one goes deeper (as seen in the *Abhidhamma* scriptures) to discover that beneath the stratum of the five aggregates there are more fundamental elements of mind and body – almost like atoms of consciousness (and below this, *emptiness*). After we have reached past the bottom layer and grasped the emptiness of all things, then we return to the daily life with new eyes. We no longer see the layers of metaphysical, political, and ethnic nonsense that have accumulated like barnacles on the man in front of us. We don't worry about his soul, or his party, or his skin color, we just see that he suffers and needs help. We respond with compassion.

Pious Jack

There's a funny scene in Jack Kerouac's *The Dharma Bums*, when he first meets Japhy Ryder (Gary Snyder). For Kerouac, Gary Snyder, who was studying the Zen lunatic masters, was "the number one *Dharma* Bum of them all." They met in 1955 and hit it off immediately, in part because they shared a love of Buddhism. Kerouac says, "We had the same favorite Buddhist saint, too: Avalokitesvara" (also known as Guanyin in China and Kwannon in Japan). Kerouac was impressed with Snyder because he knew the details of Tibetan, Chinese, Mahayana, Hinayana, Japanese, and even Burmese Buddhism, "but," he added, "I warned him at once I didn't give a goddamn about the mythology and all the names and national flavors of Buddhism, but was just interested in the first [Buddha's] four noble truths."

Kerouac remained devoted to the ethics of Buddhism – the cultivation of compassion – for his entire life (at least on paper). And he saw it as not just consistent with, but the same thing as, Catholic charity (which he imbibed with his mother's milk). He playfully teased Gary Snyder, by calling his form of *dharma* "a lot of silly Zen Buddhism." And he explained to Snyder, "I'm not a Zen Buddhist, I'm a serious Buddhist, I'm an old fashioned dreamy" sort of Buddhist.

Kerouac was raised Catholic and, despite his serious admiration for Buddhism, he always maintained a respect and awe for the saints of Christianity. He repeatedly connects Buddhist and Christian empathy in his writings, sometimes even mocking his own naiveté. In *The Dharma Bums*, after he shares some bread and wine with an older hobo, he says, "I reminded myself of the line in the *Diamond Sutra* that says, 'Practice charity without holding in mind any conceptions about charity, for charity after all is just a word.' I was very devout in those days and was practicing my religious devotions almost to perfection … . But then I really believed in the reality of charity and kindness and humility and zeal and neutral tranquility and wisdom and ecstasy." Allen Ginsberg corroborates the devotion of Kerouac during this period, claiming that it was around this time when Kerouac was regularly singing the Buddhist prayer of Three Refuges (in Buddhism the Three Refuges, or Triple

Gems, are the Buddha himself, the *dharma* or the teachings, and the *sangha* or monastic community).

The crux of Kerouac's objection to Zen was that it had left behind the kindness and compassion of Buddhism, and focused instead on the intellectual puzzles, or *koans* (e.g., What is the sound of one hand clapping?, etc.)."It's mean," Kerouac complained. "All those Zen Masters throwing young kids in the mud because they can't answer their silly word questions."

Like most Zen practitioners, Gary Snyder was only amused by this critique, not wounded by it. Zen, after all, prides itself on unflappability and celebrates the spontaneous absurdity of the present moment. After Kerouac describes the famous poetry-slam at Gallery Six, the night Allen Ginsberg read his poem "Howl," he says that all the Beats ended up at a San Fran Chinatown restaurant – fumbling chopsticks, laughing, and "yelling conversation in the middle of the night." Kerouac stumbled over to an old Chinese cook and asked him, "Why did Bodhidharma come from the West?" (The question refers to the legendary Master Bodhidharma who came to China from India in the fifth century CE – bringing Chan or Zen Buddhism with him).

"'I don't care,' said the old cook, with lidded eyes," and when Kerouac related this response to his friend Snyder,

Snyder said "Perfect answer, absolutely perfect. Now you know what I mean by Zen."

Of course, some of this is never going to make sense. It's not supposed to make sense. But part of the reason why "I don't care" is a perfect Zen answer is because Zen evolved as a reform movement in Buddhism. And as such, it sought to break entirely with the old scriptures and traditions. Zen emerges almost one thousand years after the historical Buddha lived in Northern India, and it sought to peel away all the dogmatic accretions that had formed on the *dharma*. It did this purifying by deliberately focusing on meditation only (Chan/ Zen just means meditation). Everything else in Buddhism, the ethics, metaphysics, and devotional traditions, were all jettisoned. Zen says "I don't care" about tradition, about history, about theory. But Zen retains the Stoic aspect of Buddhism – the view that one should rigorously discipline one's wanting mind.

Detaching from one's craving is not an easy task, of course, and all forms of Buddhism share a common dedication to discipline. But Gary Snyder's Zen and Ginsberg's later Tantric explorations (with "crazy wisdom" master Chogyam Trungpa) demonstrate how Buddhism "makes peace" with the body. The Buddha, recall, tried the hardcore asceticism of his Jain contemporaries, and rejected it – arguing for moderation of bodily pleasure, rather than extermination or negation. But Kerouac's Catholicism seems lurking in the background of his *dharma* interests. In the mid-1950s his notebooks include lists to remind himself to practice greater abstinence: "No chasing after women anymore. No more drunkenness or alcohol." Obviously he failed to enact Buddhist, or any other brand, of discipline on his own drinking habits, but my point is that he always preferred, despite his excellent counterculture credentials, a more conservative form of Buddhism.

There is a humorous scene in *The Dharma Bums* when Gary Snyder shows up with a beautiful woman, who strips naked in front of a disbelieving Kerouac and Ginsberg. Snyder and the girl demonstrate the Yabyum, as he calls it – a Tibetan expression for the lotus-position sexual union of a Buddhist deity and his consort (frequently depicted in Buddhist art and meant to symbolize the union of wisdom and compassion and the overcoming of the subject/object illusion). The Tantric demonstration turns into an orgy, which Ginsberg joins without anxiety but Kerouac resists (though his resistance eventually fails). His character confesses trepidation. "I'd … just gone through a year of celibacy based on my feeling that lust was the direct cause of birth which was the direct cause of suffering and death and I had … come to a point where I regarded lust as offensive and even cruel."

Unlike Ginsberg and Snyder, Kerouac seemed to think about Buddhism primarily as a species of pietism. Buddhism was filtered through Western notions of sin and virtue. But, technically speaking, there are no sins in Buddhism, not in the sense of violations of divine prohibitions. Partly this is because there is no God or Brahman to dispense binding rules, but more interestingly this is because ethics is couched within the wider framework of the pursuit of freedom, or *nibbana*. Activities and life choices are always weighed pragmatically as to whether they contribute to or detract from suffering (*dukkha*), and the answer to that evaluation is largely relative to who is asking. Activities themselves, whether they be helping old ladies across the street or selling your body for money, are neither good nor bad. They are inherently value-neutral, they just *are*. The activity becomes "bad" only if you become attached to it, only if you find yourself "needing" it and obsessing about it and not being able to be content without it. Even helping old ladies across the street can become "bad" if you become sanctimo- niously righteous about it and stake out cross-walks to get your pious "fix." So, too, sex for money is problematic when either the sex or the money becomes an addiction, but not before that. This means that there is no commandment list of *absolutely* wrong things in Buddhism, and while sexual desire and drugs and greed might trap you in this world of suffering, so might rigid religiosity and moral righteousness.

"Crazy Wisdom" and Artistic Consciousness

Taken to an extreme, the "crazy wisdom" tradition, which Allen Ginsberg eventually embraced, celebrates this idea that there is no sin in Buddhism. If sex is a transcendent act that destroys the ego temporarily in the "little death" of orgasm, then why not make use of it as a kind of meditation? This idea, admittedly not a mainstream Buddhist doctrine, is nonetheless a very old Tantric tradition. But in 1970 Tibetan master Chogyam Trungpa moved to the States and began opening meditation centers, eventually creating the Naropa University in Colorado. Trungpa's unorthodox Buddhism appealed to Ginsberg, who ended up teaching at Naropa. Far from Kerouac's moral version of Buddhism, Trungpa introduced an almost Dionysian element – a Buddhist monk who got drunk regularly, ate meat, and encouraged naked parties. The goal of this chaos was to break down the mind's urge to classify, organize, discriminate, and judge. The craziness of Trungpa was intended to shock people out of their preconceptions and to get them to accept the present moment (which has no intrinsic moral structure) and to decenter the ego.

Ginsberg found this Tantric tradition exhilarating. Despite the fact that Ginsberg, in 1974, named a Naropa department after his late friend – the Jack Kerouac School of Disembodied Poetics – one gets the feeling that Kerouac would have been uncomfortable by the Tantric approach of hippy-era Buddhism. But perhaps that was Ginsberg's inside joke when he named the school "disembodied" – for that implies not only a positive universal mind notion, but also an insinuation about sexual repression and asceticism of the body.

Other ecstasy-seeking American artists, from Jim Morrison to the Red Hot Chilli Peppers, have sought to unleash the Dionysian detonation. Whether it's sex, drugs, rock'n'roll, or meditation, the goal is to go behind phenomena, to go beyond the dominion of forms and experience the aboriginal ecstasy. That act, of exploding the ego-consciousness and even entity-consciousness, is thought to have a rejuvenating effect on us when we return to mundane consciousness. Conservative Buddhism is suspicious of intoxication, and with good reason. But the "crazy wisdom" Buddhist tradition is more uniquely allied with the arts. Even in the West, Plato says, "the man in control of his senses knocks in vain on poetry's door," and Aristotle informs us that "no great genius has ever existed without a dash of lunacy."

Consciousness and Compassion

Two threads of Buddhism seem to weave throughout the Beat scene, the hippie scene, and the contemporary artistic scene: first, its unique vision of consciousness, and second, its ethical philosophy of compassion. Even in our contemporary music scene we find artists stressing one thread rather than the other; Laurie Anderson, for example,strikes me as a Buddhist artist who is largely concerned with consciousness in her work, while Adam Yauch of the Beastie Boys and Rivers Cuomo of Weezer are more concerned with the ethical dimensions of Buddhism in their art. The philosophical connection of these two threads can be glimpsed in Kerouac's translation of the *Lankavatara Sutra*: "you yield yourself up to all beings for the sake of their eventual emancipation – you have no more desires, passions, make no more discriminations, and patiently accept that you have no more ego than the moon reflected in the water" (in *Some of the Dharma*).

Mindfulness (*sati*) is the main goal of Buddhist meditation. It is a state of egoless awareness. For some, like the practitioners of Zazen (sitting meditation) mindfulness will be a quiet affair, but for others (Trungpa's "crazy wisdom" tradition) it will be Dionysian in nature. It's ecstasy either way.

Let's remind ourselves of the purpose of mindful training. First, it is the freedom from unhealthy attachments to anxieties – simply put, peace of mind. But also, in mindfulness, one begins to realize that the ego (the self) is a habitual fiction – it doesn't really exist, so stop acting in a self-ish manner. Contrary to your everyday consciousness, you are not a stable being that exists through the past, present, and future moments, you are just a temporary aspect of the flow of becoming. Belief in a self (an essential soul), for Buddhists, is what causes us to strive to profit our selves and injure others – causes us to treat others as a mere *means* rather than as ends in themselves.

The Buddha, in the *Samyutta Nikaya* (35.206), offers a simile of "The Six Animals." Imagine, he says, that your six senses (remember that the mind is also considered a sense in Buddhism) are like six different animals: a snake, crocodile, bird, dog, hyena, and monkey. Imagine now that each animal is bound on its own rope-leash, but all of the ropes are tied together in a central knot. Each of these animals has its own respective habitat, to which it will attempt to return. The crocodile will struggle to get to the water, the bird to the air, the monkey to the forest, and so on. But when the animals become exhausted and can no longer struggle, they will submit and surrender to whichever animal happens to be strongest on that day. This, according to the Buddha, is what it's like to live without mindfulness. Our senses are drawn toward their particular pleasures and we haphazardly pursue whatever is momentarily strongest. We are locked in an internal struggle – a roped-up, six-animal "tug of war."

The solution, according to the Buddha, is to live in the present without attachment and slavery to sensual and intellectual cravings. He says that you should take your six animals and tether them to a strong stake or pole. In this way, they will still struggle for their respective pleasures, but they will grow tired and then stand, sit, or lie down right there next to the stake. The discipline and restraint of mindfulness brings this peacefulness, this equanimity.

Buddhism and the Outcasts

For many of the Beats, poetry itself is a kind of mindful meditation. Most of them agreed that art is a therapeutic process. But is the therapy designed to celebrate the self or annihilate the self? There is a Romantic strain in the Beat ethos – one that always accompanies bohemian cultures no matter what decade or century. It's this Romantic tendency to celebrate the individual and see art as narcissistic expression (i.e., the misunderstood genius) that makes an uneasy partner with the Buddhist strain in Beat culture – a strain that tries to root out and dissolve the ego into emptiness (*sunyata*).

Before there were Beats, there were many bohemians who took pleasure in laughing at the squares. Literary examples abound, like Herman Hesse's *Steppenwolf* as well as the existential slackers. Consider more pessimistic proto-Beats, like Friedrich Nietzsche and André Gide. Bohemians are generally easy to spot. They wear a seemingly effortless wardrobe (which is actually quite studied), they tend toward intellectualism, melancholy, and art. They lead unconventional sexual lives, reject the pursuit of money, and generally find solidarity through a mutual disgust with the bourgeoisie. As Gustave Flaubert once said, "Hatred of the bourgeoisie is the beginning of wisdom."

Bohemian subcultures reverse the usual value system. They reject worldly success (the recognition of respectable people and the acquisition of wealth) in favor of inner fulfillment (artistic and intellectual sensitivity). They'd rather be starving artists than comfortable bureaucrats. Sometimes, like in the Romantic era, the bohemian impulse is against rationality, which is characterized as a tyrannical force. Sometimes, like in the case of Socrates (a very early bohemian), the status quo is critiqued and resisted from the liberating vantage point of rationality. We already saw, for example, how Gautama used reason and experience to throw doubt on the Indian caste system.

Obviously the Buddha's rejection of caste was very appealing to me as a young rebel. Teen angst makes one identify with the outcasts in any story, so Buddha's rebellion was an inspiration on that front. One of the things that Buddhism and Beat culture have in common is the bohemian celebration of the *outcast*, the loser, the outsider. This is not exclusive to Buddhism, of course, since Christianity, too, celebrates the underdog (i.e., blessed are the poor, the meek, etc.). Society persecutes, or at least scoffs at, the misunderstood artist. Bohemian ideologies like Buddhism and Beat philosophy offer a welcome refuge to those of us who don't quite "fit in." Artists, who are not particularly interested in material wealth, are bound to connect with Buddhism on these grounds as well.

Critical and Creative Buddhism

I recently asked the prince of *dharma* bums, Gary Snyder, who is now a professor at the University of California, Davis, about his original attraction to Buddhism.

"Buddhism is not monotheistic. In the least." Snyder told me. "Traditional folk Buddhism remained open to the ideas of animistic spirits and miscellaneous deities in a light and playful way. It is constantly affirming pluralism. 'Beings are numberless, I vow to enlighten them / obstacles are countless, I vow to cut them down / *Dharma*-gates are limitless, I vow to enter them / The Buddha-way is endless, I vow to follow through.' It's all plural. It's not God is One, the Truth is One, there's only One Way, etc."

This pluralism was a major attraction for Snyder, and unlike the more urban-based Beat writers, Snyder grew up in close contact with nature (in a logging family) so the ecology of Buddhism appealed to him as well. "What drew me first to Buddhism, as a teenager," he explained, "was the first precept. *Ahimsa*, nonharming, in regard to all beings (not just 'thou shalt not kill other people'). I was engaged with the questions and problems of the natural world from early on."

Reflecting on this precept further, Snyder explained why he thought Buddhism appealed to so many of his Beat peers. "My generation saw the cold war, nuclear armaments, consumer greediness, profit-motive globalizing corporations, and environmental destruction – all on a steady rising curve – and found a teaching [in Buddhism] of simplicity and practice that affirmed the variety and richness of the universe."

In this description, Snyder emphasizes the Buddhist thread of compassion and ethics, but his own Zen poetry also explores the thread of Buddha consciousness. In addition to creating mental composure, Buddhism acknowledges that *conceptual thought* is a bounded domain inside a larger territory of meaning. Aesthetic meaning, which is more sensual, imaginative, and perceptual, is another domain inside this larger territory.

The early Buddhism of Gautama has the more rational and even *critical* quality that I've been praising throughout this book. It sees itself as dismantling earlier Hindu mistakes – errors that lead to alienation (e.g., the caste system) and errors that lead to continued suffering (e.g., an immortality-craving religious metaphysics). Beat writers appreciated some of this, especially the counterculture revolutionary stuff, but they seemed to gravitate more toward later Buddhism (Mahayana).

By comparison with the earlier critical orientation, Mahayana Buddhism is a tradition of *creativity*. Having won its battles against the essentialist metaphysics of Vedanta, Buddhism in Tibet and China became much more imaginative, inventive, and artistic. Mahayana scriptures like the *Lankavatara* and *Diamond Sutras*, some of Kerouac's favorites, explicitly move beyond the critical phase – which they deride as the "reasoning knowledge of the philosophers" – and embrace, instead, a more gnostic, almost secret, form of mystical intuition. It's this later stuff that tends to feed into the quantum mysticism movement that we looked at in the previous chapter.

Emptiness, for example, became a major aspect of later Chinese and Tibetan Buddhism, even though it has roots in Indian Hinayana. Indian philosophers like Nagarjuna (c. 150–250 CE) had argued that all dichotomies of thinking (e.g., us or them, good or bad, being or not-being, etc.) are illusions of the conventional mind. But this had special resonance for Chinese philosophers, whose indigenous

Daoism had celebrated a deeper unity beneath the opposites of yin and yang. Beats like Kerouac, Snyder, and Ginsberg were all excited by this aspect of Buddhism because, among other things, it provided a foundation for doing poetry in the first place. Our ordinary way of thinking and operating in the world assumes that our conscious minds reflect the real world – the mind discriminates differences because there are differences out there in nature. Buddhism comes along and says that these discriminations are just illusions of the mind (fabrications) and do not reflect reality – which is "empty" (without inherent form). Consequently, according to this school of Buddhism, *literal* language (like that practiced in everyday speech and the sciences) cannot access reality. But poetry can. The unexpected twist of the elegant haiku, for example, can suddenly reveal a nondiscursive truth that no literal language can represent. The Beats generally agreed with this skepticism about literal language, and saw it as a validation and motivation for doing poetry.

Truth in Art

Ecstasy, according to this tradition, is a better guide to truth and reality than rational thought. The association of *ecstasy* in music and art, and the same kind of experience in the spiritual traditions, is well known. The ecstatic experience, or peak experience, or oceanic feeling, can be accessed via several different pathways – intoxicants, art, sex, religion, and so on. For me, music has always been pretty good evidence that the rational mind has its limits. Of course, it should be obvious by now that I'm not a mystic in the traditional sense. I don't agree with most mystics, who hold that reason takes us only so far and then art and religion take us on to a higher realm. Art and religion are not absolutely privileged forms of knowing – in fact, they really stink when one is trying to predict, understand, and heal the human body, for example. Medicine makes religion look downright silly in certain situations. But art is equally powerful and even superior to reason *in certain situations*. Imagination and art seem much better, for example, in touching and even educating our moral sensibility. And in that magical moment of playing music, especially improvisational music, you can also discover hidden parts of yourself – territories that are usually obscured by the internal chatter of one's discursive mind. But the additional virtue of ensemble music is that one can communicate (non-verbally and nonconceptually) with the other players and the audience. So there's a profound sense of community that emerges during such musical experiences.

For Jack Kerouac and many other Beats, the ecstatic melody squealed forth from the horns of Charlie Parker, Dizzy Gillespie, and the all the architects of bebop. Bop, according to Kerouac, was the music that tapped into the secret reality underneath our phenomenal experience. Like a decoding transducer it allowed him to hear behind the matrix, to the hidden logic of zeros and ones – the "emptiness of forms," as he liked to say. Poetry was another method – the one that bonded all the Beats – for transcending the little self.

After Charlie Parker, Jimi Hendrix seemed to do the same thing for the following generation – namely, push beyond the matrix. And in my own generation we lacked the piercing arrow-tip of such instrumental virtuosos, but made up for it with whole genres, like punk, grunge, and hip-hop, which sought to unmask hypocrisy and reveal at least the next exploitative level down beneath daily experience.

Art seeks to liberate or emancipate us. Sometimes the oppressor is political, and sometimes it is our own inner cravings. Art both shows us the error of our ways and gives us a promising glimpse of our hidden potentialities. Buddhism, then, *is* an artform – not that different from painting or playing an instrument. It has its own craft, method, and ritual, but Buddhism like art seeks to construct meaning in our lives. And it is not satisfied to take whatever meaning is already present – the world of suffering that we're born into. With mindfulness, Buddhism gives us the tools to attain illumination and to actively construct new meaning.

Chapter VI

Work: Wealth and Worth

"Alright," he said, inhaling deeply, "you take the machete and follow behind me. I'm gonna use the axe to take down the bigger stuff." My father looked at the sky to measure how much time we had before we'd be in pitch-black Wisconsin night. We had to leave enough time to build a fire, or we'd be in bad shape for dinner.

"Why don't we wait until the chainsaw is fixed?" I protested feebly.

"No," he snapped, "I want to clear this path to the river before your mother arrives tomorrow. Besides," he paused, looking at me like *I* was the one who was ridiculous, "do you got somethin' better to do?"

"Well," I risked, "didn't we clear a perfectly good path yesterday, not fifty yards from here?" He started to hunch over some thick weed tangle, and before he attacked it with his axe he said the thing I'd heard him say a million times.

"We didn't do it *right* the first time," he resolved, "so, we're doin' it *again*. Capice?"

After about two hours of hacking and slashing our way through saplings, reeds, and shrubbery, my arm muscles were burning, my head was pounding, and a good pint of my 12-year-old blood had been drained by the hinterland's finest mosquitoes. It was a typical weekend at "the property" – a scruffy, useless, patch of five acres in northern cheese country, too hilly and wooded to develop in any useful way. And yet my father, gripped by some obscure vision, apprenticed my brothers and I in the most backbreaking forest-clearing projects. One month we'd be dragging fallen trees with chains, the next month planting seedlings, then mowing down fern fields or building log bridges across the narrow river. The only goal, as far as I could tell, was that my father felt some need to leave his mark on this hopeless five-acre thicket. If I had known about Sisyphus at that age, my brothers and I would have nicknamed my dad.

Even though, to this day, none of us knows why we were manicuring a jungle, my brothers and I all learned something important about work – something all of us have retained decades later: do it *right*, or do it *again* until it is right, and do it with everything you got.

My father was a steel worker and my mother was a nurse. I had a blue-collar upbringing. Perhaps my intimate history with manual labor actually inspired me to pursue a decidedly nonmanual academic career. As a laborer, I've washed dishes, stripped and waxed floors, painted houses, stocked shelves, unloaded trucks, chopped down trees, built decks, assembled tables, repaired Xerox machines, framed pictures, cleaned schools and churches, played music in bars, weddings, and theaters – then, gradually, graded papers, gave lectures, researched, and wrote.

Whether you're a manual laborer, an information laborer, an entertainer, or whatever, there are some universals to the working life. Buddhist strategies, like mindfulness, eon perspective, and ego reduction, are often very valuable as we deal with these universal work challenges. For example, most of us find ourselves in a *hierarchic* social relationship at work – some people are below us on the ladder and some are above us. We have to navigate, sometimes with breathtaking dexterity, the many power relations at work. Another universal aspect of working life is that you probably work with some *idiots*. Perhaps they flounder around below you in the hierarchy, and you have to follow after them, cleaning up their various messes. Or they're perched above you on the ladder and you have to take whatever abuse they hurl downward. Less obvious, perhaps, is the fact that sometimes *you* are that idiot.

Other universal challenges include mind-numbing boredom, high-stress performance anxiety, fatigue, busybody gossiping, addiction to drama, overambition, fears of being laid off, bureaucratic alienation, and so on. And work has the added stress of being the place where you tend to search for both *wealth* and *worth*. You chase the paycheck, try to provide for your family, and search for that elusive prosperity and purchasing power, but you also seek recognition, respect, acknowledgment, appreciation, and, in some cases, reputation, fame, and even celebrity. What follows, then, are some Buddhist strategies – all tested by yours truly – for attaining some shred of inner peace in the workplace and the world of status.

Neutralizing Bullies at Work

First, let's dispatch the bullies. Every workplace has them. And truth be told, much of the Buddhist advice here could be applied profitably to school life as well, where bullying can be intense. But since school kids are probably not buying my book, I'll leave it to you, dear reader, to impart this stuff to the adolescent demographic.

Neutralizing bullies is within your power. Some people have *actual* enemies in life – people who want to do them harm for one reason or another. If you haven't had this sort of experience, try not to judge those who have. This sort of enemy exists in most war-torn regions, for example, where histories of offense and vengeance turn people against each other in a seemingly terminal and absolute way. Inner-city gang warfare fits this description as accurately as any of the conflict regions around the globe. Enemies also exist in our personal lives, usually fashioned out of domestic humiliation and feelings of revenge. Crime stats, no matter where you are on the globe, reveal plentiful encounters between domestic enemies. Outside these conflicts, you can even have an unrelated insane person simply *imagine* that you are his enemy, and just like that, you now have a real enemy. But most of us, thankfully, encounter our enemies as much less virulent workplace characters. They're not out to dance on our graves or add us to their victim tattoos, but they are serious drags on our personal buoyancy and our ability to get things done.

The loud, red-faced, vein-popping asshole is just the most obvious workplace bully. To his battery of assault weapons, we must add the more covert and insidious machinations of the quiet manipulator, the mid-level take-it-out-on-you authoritarian, the character assassination specialist, the passive-aggressive feel-sorry-for-me mastermind, and other intimidators, browbeaters, oppressors, and tormentors.

Buddhism offers the same seemingly impossible advice that many other religions offer – meet your enemies with love, because love conquers hate. What?! Oh brother, you're saying to yourself. I could have gone to a fortune cookie for that kind of wisdom! True, this is the familiar paradox of most religious ethics, but in Buddhism the meaning is different. We are not encouraged to "turn the other cheek" so we'll get some reward in Heaven. That doesn't even make sense in Buddhism.

In the *Dhammapada*, the Buddha articulates a pragmatic form of this teaching. "'He insulted me, he hurt me, he defeated me, he robbed me.' Those who think such thoughts will not be free from hate. Those who do *not* harbor such thoughts will be free from hate. For hate is not conquered by hate. Hate is conquered by love" (I.3–5).

The translation here is misleading. The ancient Pali word, often translated as "love," is *metta*, which more accurately means "care," "goodwill," "kindness." This does not mean that the next time your bullying boss rips you a new one at work, you should give him a big hug. It just means that you do not respond with fire, both internally and externally. The Buddha says, "I will endure words that hurt in silent peace as the strong elephant endures arrows in battle, for many people lack self-control" (*Dhammapada* XXIII.320).

Abuse surely triggers feelings and thoughts in me, but suffering is subjective and I know I can extinguish the flames of hostility before they take over. If I don't feel genuine kindness (*metta*) toward the bully who's browbeating me, that's understandable – but I can still *act* as if I feel it. There's nothing disingenuous about this. We're so hung up by our Romantic ideas about acting from our authentic feelings, and expressing ourselves authentically, that we forget how new habits of behavior can slowly transform our internal habits of the heart. Act calm and peaceful repeatedly, and eventually you start to feel calm and peaceful. It takes great discipline to act magnanimously and even kindly toward an idiot who is venting spleen on you, but here's why you should do it.

First, you turn your mind into a Teflon surface that disallows contamination from outside aggression. For Buddhism, happiness and virtue are internal states of health, and this inner harmony is an end in itself rather than a means to some end. Getting your head bit off at work is humiliating and painful, but compare it with the seemingly infinite ways that your own feelings of vengeance and anger can burn inside you. Okay, your bully co-worker is a nuisance, but now your own cravings for revenge are keeping you awake all night, ruining your weekends, bleeding over into your family relations, and so on. Some of the techniques that allow you to conquer the inner hate are ones we've already talked about, like eon perspective – taking a long-range view of your troubles and remembering that all things must pass. But other techniques seem especially helpful at the workplace, like responding to anger with humor. Laughing when someone thinks you should be cowering is both exhilarating and effective as a message to your assailant. Moreover, everyone knows that bullies are deeply neurotic, insecure, and fearful people, so *pity* is a more fitting response to someone who is essentially a child in an adult's body. Everyone who works with a bully probably knows enough about her sad personal life to feel confident that her suffering is way worse than yours, so compassion is a more appropriate response.

I once saw Vietnamese monk Thich Nhat Hanh, at a lecture, offer a helpful metaphor for handling difficult people. When you plant lettuce, he said, you don't blame the lettuce if it doesn't grow well. Instead, you look for reasons why it is not doing well. The plant may need more sun, or fertilizer, or water, or whatever. It would be odd to blame the lettuce. So, too, when people are hostile to you, you should try to understand what circumstances have led them to this unfortunate state.

Now if it was only this reason, of inner equanimity, that justified "keeping cool" in the face of torment, then it might be tantamount to recommending that we resign ourselves to "doormat" status. But here's the other dimension of Buddhist kindness. When you respond with kindness, or noble spirit, you actually improve your enemy in the transaction. First, you demonstrate to the bully (and anybody else in the room) that you are untouched by his wrath.

When I was younger, I once had a co-worker bully me into all manner of activities I did not agree with, and he did this by appealing to my need to be liked by others. He would invent gossip and come to me stealthily like a confidant reporting that people were talking and saying I lacked integrity if I didn't do x, y, and z (and, of course, x, y, and z were just the things that the bully wanted done). He knew I wanted people to think well of me, and he used it repeatedly to manipulate me. In time, I actually outgrew this desire for other people's approval – which is, by the way, a highly liberating bit of maturity. And one day he approached me with Oscar-winning melodrama about the inevitable disappointment of my peers, should I fail to act according to his plan. I turned to him with real sincerity and quietly said, "My colleagues' opinions about my character mean less than zero to me." He was utterly deflated by this and truly shocked. He never bothered me again, because I had removed the "handle" on myself that he always used to shake me up and down.

I had another bully choose a public forum to suggest that I was an incompetent boob. I was speaking to large group, and I felt myself go red and tasted the anger in the back of my throat. But I smiled and said, "Well, I defer to your expertise in this matter, and I look to you now for some wisdom." I sat down to wait. I don't usually say the right thing at the right time, but I could not have been more successful on that day. The bully floundered and dithered in a desperate attempt to regain the upper hand – the position of power – but now, seated and composed, I was demonstrably untouchable.

One of the great literary bullies of the twentieth century is the character Jack from William Golding's *The Lord of the Flies*. This pubescent menace frightens, pummels, and manipulates every other castaway kid on the island, until he has them all under his control. The novel is about the staggering potential for aggression inside all of us. But Golding offers us a subtle yet powerful episode where Jack is utterly neutralized by one of his usual whipping-boys. The character Simon is detached about his own desires, and when Jack tries to manipulate the starving boys by controlling who gets pig meat from the hunt, Simon disempowers Jack by giving away his own portion to another kid. Jack is bewildered by this and emasculated. It doesn't exactly turn Jack into a better person, but if enough kids followed Simon's lead of nonviolent resistance, then the dynamic might have unfolded quite differently.

Obviously, there's a limit to the cool forbearance of Buddhism. If someone should threaten you in a dangerous fashion, then the proper Buddhist response would be to (very mindfully) punch their lights out. Self-defense – just as much as nonviolent resistance – is entirely within the bounds of

Buddhist philosophy, otherwise there would be no such thing as Kung Fu. But in most workplace situations, this is not an issue, and self-control is more appropriate and effective.

The enemy is improved or instructed by your kind response because he learns, painfully, that he does not have power over you. This is a good lesson for all manipulators to learn. And lastly, your kindness has the added benefit of acting as an inspiration to the bully – a model, if you will, for how the bully might also attain some share of this imperturbable happiness. Buddhism suggests that eventually haters will come to the conclusion that "if I can't beat 'em, then I'll join 'em." People who demonstrate noble kindness are rare. But if you've seen people do it, then you can attest to the fact that they seem filled with vitality, strength, and even joy. Who doesn't want to get a little bit of that in their own lives?

Spinoza noticed the same thing and gave the same reasons for recommending the goodwill strategy. "He who lives according to the guidance of reason strives, as far as he can, to repay the other's hate, anger, and disdain toward him, with love or nobility" (*Ethics* IV.46). To hate someone is to imagine him, incorrectly, as the cause of one's sadness. And, making this mistake, I will be tempted to remove or destroy that person. But this is like confusing a symptom with a disease. And Spinoza, like the Buddha, adds that a kind and noble person will be more joyful (because joy is a harmonic state of the healthy psyche), so such a person will be more powerful and effective in pursuit of his goals.

And Then There's the Work Itself

This brings us to another aspect of Buddhism and work. Bullies, bosses, employees, and everybody else aside, there's the work itself. Whatever it is you happen to do, whether it's giving haircuts or running a country, you have to decide whether you will do it well or not. Many times, when I was working lame jobs for companies I didn't care about, I'd slowly slouch toward idleness and lethargy. The company doesn't know I exist, I'm utterly expendable, my labor goes unnoticed, I can't even afford the product I'm working on, I don't respect the management, and so on. Most of us have had this experience, and it transforms work into unqualified drudgery.

Buddhism, however, asks us to bracket out all those considerations – some of which may be entirely true – and asks us instead to focus on the task at hand, no matter how trivial it seems. If mindfulness (*sati*) can transform the simple act of sitting and breathing into an artform that nourishes the mind and body, then imagine what it can do with work. Bringing ourselves back to the activity at hand is especially hard if we're folding pants at the Gap, or flipping burgers at McDonalds, or doing the accounting at Exxon Mobil. The tendency is always to focus forward in time toward the future, when we will get off work, or get our paycheck, or get our promotion, or whatever. For many of us, work is the time we spend *waiting to live*. But if you can sink down and be more present in your activity, then you will discover the subtle joys of quality labor and the oblique happiness that comes from accomplishing something with excellence.

I'm not naive. Your job cleaning septic tanks might be loathsome to you and you might be right to type up some new resumes, but let's acknowledge that there's an excellent way to clean those tanks and a half-assed way to do it. I learned this from my dad, who taught me how to wax floors, use a machete, clean a toilet, and wire an outlet. The benefit of approaching work with mindful effort, care, and skill is that the work then changes (even if only for a few hours) from a *means to an end* to an *end in itself*. Carefully tuning a piano, for example, that no one will hear or appreciate can still be a deeply rewarding achievement. Or consider manicuring a lawn that will only grow back. And labor that has no *global* meaning or deep significance can still have profound *local* meaning and value.

Buddhist mindfulness suggests that you try to work with dedication, grace, and style – like you're on stage at Carnegie

Hall, even when you're just tightening lug-nuts on wheel studs. Attention to detail and thoroughness are virtues in the working life – whatever your vocation. The Buddha says. "The monk who has the joy of watchfulness and who looks with fear on thoughtlessness, he goes on his path like a fire, burning all obstacles both great and small" (*Dhammapada*, II.31).

Buddhism, especially Zen, believes that if you're gonna do something, anything really, then do it well. But it is silly to ignore some basic facts about our modern working world of alienated labor. If your work demands so little of your abilities that a chimp with a hammer could do the same job effectively, then you can't solve this problem by forcing yourself to "be here now" all the time. It seems reasonable for you to want to "be somewhere else now." So, there has to be some *Middle Way* here too. The Zensters think you can make *anything*, including assembly-line repetition, into fulfilling meditation. Instead, I recommend some job that meets you halfway, by posing some real challenges for you to actualize your potential.

And Money ...

Another undeniable aspect of our modern working world is that we don't live in a barter system, we live in a capital, or money, system. In ancient times, and in some contemporary communities, we might just trade our skilled labor – I'm a good cobbler and you make good arrows, so let's swap things. Or I'm a good hunter and you're a good healer, so let's swap skills or competencies. That's not our world, and it hasn't been for a long time. We work for money, and money is wealth. Property is wealth, too, but only insofar as it is fungible with money. Money can be exchanged for almost anything. The commodities, services, and sensual pleasures of life are limited only by the amount of your coin.

So unless you were born into a rich family, work is your only real method for the procurement of wealth. Now Buddhism is austere, but not like some other ascetic traditions (like Jainism). The Buddha recommended the Middle Way because real happiness comes with comparatively low-level prosperity and comfort. Like Epicurus in the West, the Buddha claimed that it is better to train oneself to enjoy simple foods rather than fine gourmet meals, because economic, political, and even weather changes could suddenly rob us of our exotic spices and delicacies. If we had allowed ourselves to become attached to such connoisseur pleasures, then we will suffer in ways that could have been avoided. We are advised to focus on more stable and reliable sources of happiness: simple fare, friendships, family, and intellectual cultivation. There is nothing inherently wrong with certain foods, pleasures, or even wealth itself. There are only problems of attachment. So, let's be clear, Buddhism does not want you to be poor. Remember that after his big-pimpin' days in the lap of luxury, Gautama tried and rejected poverty as a life strategy. Moderation is the successful path.

But since money, in our culture, is the means by which we attain most of our goals – not just consumer goods, but also travel, or college for our kids, or even art appreciation – then it seems to us that we can never have enough of it. Money is potentiality. So the dangers of craving (*tanha*) are palpable around the issue of money, and money itself is a primer-pump for zombie levels of appetite. We chase the money, and the money chases the stuff. I'm not on a soapbox here. I struggle with this daily.

Look around at the more devoted money chasers among your acquaintances. Just below their surface, you will notice that they are running scared. They are running scared with good reason. If you make affluence your goal in life, or even if you keep telling yourself that your substantial savings is still not enough, then you will be perpetually restless and stressed. More important, despite all the rhetoric and sloganeering to the contrary, career expansion almost always costs something on the home front. Generating income takes time and energy, but you've only got a finite amount of time and energy. Even if you cut the television and the sleeping times down, and maybe substitute smoking for eating, your friendships and your family time will still suffer.

Many people eventually just give up entirely on things like family and friends. Some money chasers are very lonely people, even amid the hustle and bustle of their pursuit. Watch as some people squirm to avoid the utterly frightening *empty moment* when they have to sit quietly with themselves – and this is especially acute in our technology-connected world of iPods, cell phones, personal organizers, personal gaming devices, and so on. One reason why money chasers are running scared is because they know deep down that if they fall on hard times, there won't be anybody there to help them. Community is something that must be fostered, and if you haven't cultivated one, then you cannot avail yourself of its supportive powers. Money makes the illusion of self-sufficiency more persuasive, and we are lured into the erroneous belief that we are independent, autonomous, free, and sovereign. But Buddhism disagrees, and stresses the inter-dependence of all humans, indeed all beings.

The Oblivion Bubble

Money and the things it buys are some of the most obvious cases of impermanent reality. But that doesn't mean it cannot be enjoyed for what it is. If work gets you wealth and wealth gets you certain kinds of enjoyments, then their impermanence does not necessarily diminish their quality – it's only by obsessing that we spoil the pleasures of wealth. And I also do not want to leave the impression that all wealthy people are lonely. That is patently false and many very prosperous families are also very healthy families. But, from the Buddhist perspective, one last danger lurks inside the wealthy lifestyle. It is the danger of the oblivion bubble. Wealthy people have drivers who chauffer them around, maids who clean their homes, cooks and caterers, masseuses, and personal assistants; they swim in big pristine pools, fly to exotic golf courses or theater openings, purchase all the cutting-edge technology, and eat gourmet meals on a daily basis. The consequence of all this is that the normal gap between desire and fulfillment becomes smaller and smaller. One rarely has to stop and *delay* gratification, or more likely for the rest of us, actually admit the *impossibility* of some gratifications. My wealthy friend's son, for example, was convinced that *everybody* had a limousine chauffeur, and he was shocked to learn that my son and I were not only limo-less, but didn't own a car and walked everywhere. The same revelations occurred around issues of food, housing, play, and all such quotidian matters. In even the best-intentioned and good-hearted wealthy people, a remarkable innocence evolves about the value of money.

I'm generally broke all the time, so I'm usually on the underside of this dynamic, but when I lived in Cambodia I saw, daily, what it was like to live inside an oblivion bubble. Shortly after I arrived in Cambodia, I was talking to my Khmer friend in Phnom Penh about the beautiful Angkor Wat temples in the north of the country, and he confessed sheepishly that he had never seen them and probably never would. Angkor Wat is the pride of the Khmer people, and yet this man would probably never have enough money to afford the short boat ride (a few hours) to see this temple complex. Forget about dental work, medical operations, restaurant food, a car, school, or a TV.

I wasn't dumb. I knew about Cambodian poverty in a kind of abstract way. But I had to spend a lot of time in Cambodia before I could really get a good sense of the many constraints that are born of such poverty. Here in the States, wealthy people are similarly removed and abstractly aware of poverty. Like Gautama in his father's mansion, wealthy people are oftentimes unintentionally inconsiderate – thoughtless about the world outside the bubble. This daily disconnect reduces empathy and compassion for those vast majorities out there – those people out there whom rich kids glimpse through the windows of their luxury SUVs when they momentarily turn away from their personal DVD players on their way to ride their ponies at their ranch homes.

While it is obvious that wealthy people have a shorter gap between *want* and *fulfillment*, it's also true that the machines of consumer economy want a similar shortening for all the rest of us too. It is hard to be happy with less, as Buddhism recommends, when advertising and marketing are always inventing new ways to breach our defenses. Corporate stores, like grocery chains, for example, have long tracked our tastes and preferences by giving each of us a discount card and then storing our purchases in digital databanks. And as we browse the Internet, for example, it has become commonplace to see ads for products that some artificial intelligence (AI) has decided that we would like. Our previous choices are stored and an algorithm finds similar items to parade before us at a later date. It's remarkable how often I am offered something I really am interested in. The accuracy is impressive. But now the AI is getting even more sophisticated. Now storewide sensors can determine when you've entered a store by detecting your discount card in your wallet, and they can track where you are moving and pausing in the aisles. TV monitors are being installed as ubiquitous features of such stores, and personalized ads for stuff you're interested in will start to appear before you as you move around the store. Some coffee shops, for example, are already employing the strategy, and if their AI detects you near the checkout and notices that you sometimes like bagels with your coffee, then glamour shots of tasty hot bagels will start to appear near the checkout monitors (see "The Way the Brain Buys," in *The Economist*, December 20, 2008). In addition, biometric facial recognition software has already been developed that can read your responses to video sales images. So, while you're watching an ad at the store, the ad is watching you. And with split-second speed, the ads are finding just the right images to pique your pleasure centers and stimulate your consumption tendencies. One of our great defense strategies for avoiding overindulgence – the out of sight, out of mind tactic – will be no longer available to us. As these insidious technologies increase, it will be interesting to see how well we can attain and maintain control over our cravings.

Our whole culture seems to run on the engine of desire. If you have only lived in the States, you may not have noticed this disturbing fact. The culture of desire is like the air we breathe, and may not seem toxic if you were raised on it. But spending time in the developing world quickly rids you of the assumption that consumption is the natural state of affairs.

In the *Anguttara Nikaya*, the Buddha offers some very practical advice, still useful, for how we might navigate our working life through the difficult path between greed, over-ambition, thoughtlessness, and other dangers. Working stiffs are called "householders" in most ancient Indian scriptures, to distinguish them and their path from monks and others. And the Buddha describes four special kinds of happiness for the householder: ownership, wealth, debtlessness, and blamelessness. The happiness of ownership is defined as "wealth acquired by energetic striving, amassed by strength of arm, won by sweat, lawful and lawfully gotten." The happiness of wealth consists in the worker both enjoying her products of wealth and also using her wealth to do meritorious deeds. In addition, there is obvious happiness to be had in being debt free, and lastly one should work such that one is blameless in action, speech, and mind (*Anguttara Nikaya*, book IV, chapter 7).

It is not enough to seek these forms of happiness in work. The Buddha makes recommendations about how we should be using our profits. Any riches attained by noble work should be used in five ways. First, one must "provide material welfare to parents, wife, children, employees, and oneself." Second, one should "provide the same for friends and companions." Third, it is important to "keep one's goods safe from bad luck, fire and water, kings and robbers, enemies," and so on. Fourth, one should use some money for the offerings to ancestors and also for the entertaining of guests. And lastly, one must use some profits to make offerings to the monks and the Buddhist community (*Anguttara Nikaya*, book V, chapter 4). The goal of these practices, like everything else in Buddhism, is to assist in the reduction of craving and the increasing of compassion. With just a little bit of tweaking, you can see how such work and wealth-related recommendations could be applied today.

A Mindful Approach to Fame and Fortune

In any case, wealth is not the only reason why people work hard, nor is it the only way to attain status in our culture. Work and wealth are definitely means by which we pursue *worth*, or social *status*. But in our society we also have a significant cult of celebrity, one that not only garners much of our free-time attention but also inspires many young people to try their luck at fame. In past eras, it seems that people strove for fame because fame produced wealth, and wealth produced all the obvious pleasures and powers. But now, with the expansion of entertainment mass-media and the glamorization of gossip, we have arrived at an era that fetishizes fame itself. Fame is not like the old status of honor or glory; in fact, people are often celebrated and media-coddled these days for dishonorable activities. And even in the fields of entertainment, the bar has been lowered significantly. Many famous entertainers work very hard, developing their talents, to achieve their high status in the public eye. But a new breed of talentless, vapid people have become wildly famous for no apparent reason, except dumb luck and the fact that the seemingly indiscriminate holy light of mass-media marketing has shined its rays upon them.

None of this would rise above the level of amusing if it weren't for the fact that many young people have fallen for the ruse. As a professor at an arts and media college, I can assure you that an increasing number of students are intoxicated by the dream of fame, because they have been tracking media-famous people all their lives. If I ask my students to name a musical pop star, or actor, or sports figure, they can spend hours ticking off a list in their heads. But if I ask them to name a single scientist, they go deadly quiet, and then one brave soul tentatively ventures a "Well, um, isn't there that one dude who's in a wheelchair, and he talks funny?" The idea of being a rock star or a hip-hop star or a movie star is obviously attractive to anybody in a certain age bracket. But, now with the advent of talentless famous people, the traditional means of attaining fame in entertainment – ability, skill, hard work – have been swept away in the minds of young wannabes.

In previous eras, there was always a tension, especially for famous people, between integrity and selling out. If an artist had high integrity, then he was usually skewered by fans if he appeared in a crass commercial context. Now, there is no real disgust for such selling out – it is considered as just another career strategy. And I don't want to sound overly critical of this trend. It might just be a more successful pragmatic move that allows an artist the economic freedom to choose real work in between dumb but profitable blockbuster projects. But let's face it, the rise of celebrity culture has altered the way we think about integrity.

Buddhism obviously recommends a life of moderation and integrity, rather than excess and empty fame. But why is hard work, craft, and presence a better pathway than seeking celebrity status – especially when you can attain the benefits of being a star without the talent part? What is the difference between pursuing excellence and pursuing enjoyment? What is the difference between appearance and reality?

I suppose a person could fake it in Buddhism, just like anything else, but it's hard to see the point. You could fake meditation, and simply give the appearance of wisdom and peace. God knows, many false gurus have gotten laid this way, or convinced scores of gullible people to hand over their property. But the whole goal of mindfulness is to eradicate our usual tendency to just "go through the motions." So is there some inherent value to the work itself, beyond the pleasurable consequences?

Working for many years as a blues musician in Chicago made me think a lot about the *veneer* of integrity versus the *substance* of it. Blues has certain similarities with Buddhism. Both are very much concerned with the problem of suffering, both seek a therapeutic approach to the psyche, and both privilege authenticity and presence over everything else. Obviously, blues and Buddhism have some major differences too – the one stirs up and exercises the emotions, while the other seeks to cool them off. But let me meditate a little, using blues, on the issues of celebrity and integrity.

The Zen of Vocation: Forget about the Groupies and Focus on the Craft

I played in blues bands for more than fifteen years, having the very good fortune to play with legends like Buddy Guy and Bo Diddley, but it wasn't until I started playing in a *rock* band that I got invited to play the House of Blues. The irony here is delicious. The House of Blues is a well known chain of clubs all over the States that purport to offer gritty blues culture, but almost never actually book blues acts on their stages – and in fairness to them, it's usually because blues artists don't draw the big numbers of fans that pop music does (and there's a lot of overhead in these Disneyfied clubs). So, one night I stood on the expansive spot-lighted stage, playing for a packed house of tourists and well-heeled yuppies, feeling a little guilty and nervous about my now teetering blues credentials. Don't get me wrong. It was sweet to play a club that actually had a glitzy dressing room, complete with sumptuous snack trays and an overstocked beer fridge. This must be what it's like to be a rock star. This is not what it's like to be a blues musician. But I could feel comfortable in this corporate setting, sucking up to Mammon, because I could console myself with the fact that our dressing-room came complete with a shower! No kidding, a shower … with stacks of immaculate white towels. The sins of my musical prostitution would be wiped clean. I could go forth purified and moisturized.

The very next day, I actually left Chicago to drive south on a pilgrimage down to blues country – Delta country. My goal was to visit the homeland of blues great Robert Johnson, and continue on down to New Orleans to finally, as Muddy Waters commands, "get me a mojo." The whole strange experience, standing on stage at the House of Blues the night before I left to explore the absurdly poor Mississippi Delta, got me thinking about authenticity, integrity, and selling out. Blues itself, like Buddhism, is a paragon of integrity, resolutely refusing to sell out. But all artists and craftspeople have struggled with these issues at one time or another, and Western culture has well-worn archetypes for this particular temptation and struggle.

Robert Johnson himself is a recent incarnation of the Faustian bargain. Born in 1911, Johnson spent most of his short life in the Delta area, where he substituted the life of the rambling blues singer for the backbreaking life of the sharecropper. In the early 1930s, when he left the area of Robinsonville for Hazelhurst, he was known only as a mediocre talent. But when he returned sometime later he was manifestly changed. He was so talented when he strolled back into town that rumors began to circulate. A story evolved that Johnson had made a deal with the devil at a desolate crossroads. Here he supposedly wagered his soul for the power to play his instrument and sing with supernatural skill. Johnson's own eerie songs "Me and the Devil," "Crossroads," and "Hell Hound on My Trail" fueled the legends. He was indeed a phenomenal finger-style and slide guitarist, a talented composer of ironic and moving songs, and a passionate singer of the blues. His work represents a kind of prism through which Delta blues passed on its way up north to the urban blues of Chicago. Contemporary blues culture still harks back to Johnson as a patron saint of all things "blue": sorrowful heartache, struttin' and gamblin', prideful self-affirmation, ramblin', and regret.

Johnson played his last gig at a juke joint named Three Forks on a Saturday night, August 13, 1938. Some say that the devil finally came to collect his debt, but most scholars agree that Johnson messed around with the wrong woman (one who had a very jealous lover) and paid the price. He died of poisoning at the age of 27.

I drove to Mississippi and spent a week hunting down

obscure geographical references that appear in Johnson's songs. Some towns were gone altogether, and others had dilapidated vestiges of earlier eras. I spent time in Rosedale, Greenvile, Robinsonville, and other tiny towns – collecting little pieces of cotton and Mississippi mud for my future mojo. I wanted to find the Three Forks joint where Robert Johnson met his Maker. I didn't find the bar, but I did find the sign that had hung above the juke-joint door.

In Clarksdale, Mississippi, there is a Delta Blues Museum that houses the historic bar sign in one of their display rooms. The director of the very modest museum sent me to the nearby corner of Highways 61 and 49. No one actually knows where Johnson's real crossroads is located, but 61/49 is the conventionally designated spot where Mississippi folks tip their hats. I found an excellent hole-in-the-wall barbecue joint on the junction of 61 and 49 called Abe's, that served no-frills rib specials, the eating of which certainly constitutes your own private deal with the devil, or at the very least it hastens the meeting with your Maker.

While I was toweling off the barbecue sauce and drinking some decidedly local beer, I stared out Abe's window at the crossroads sign. Robert Johnson is a modern-day Faust, and like Christopher Marlowe's and Johann Wolfgang von Goethe's Dr. Faust he simultaneously elicits our admiration and our reproach. The reproach is obvious, of course, and doesn't require much explanation – people who sell their souls to the devil are not the kind of people whom you want your daughter to marry. But Johnson's deal, like that of Faust before him, is not as crass and shallow as one might think. Johnson didn't make a deal to become famous. In fact, fame per se doesn't even enter into the legend or into Johnson's real life. By the time musicologists came to the Delta looking for him, he was already dead (so they found Muddy Waters instead). All Robert did was make a deal to become talented. This is very different from a wager for fame. Selling your soul to become famous or wealthy is obscene, selling your soul to become talented is strangely beautiful.

But selling your soul here is just a metaphor for the deep and profound sacrifices that craftspersons make as they try to perfect themselves and their work. This applies not just to artists per se but also to scientists, manual laborers, computer programmers, and other devotees of excellence. Our culture is understandably ambivalent about these people because we respect and love their craft, but we lament the damage that their passionate pursuits sometimes wreak on their families, friends, and even their own health. I would like to have the talent of a Van Gogh, for example, but I certainly wouldn't want to *be* Van Gogh.

At the end of Goethe's *Faust* there is a beautifully redemptive moment. After we have watched Faust do a lot of stupid stuff (facilitated, of course, by the devil Mephistopheles), we find him at death's door. He is a tragic figure because he is still striving to understand himself and the human condition, he is still struggling to grasp the deeper truths. He has made many mistakes and taken many wrong turns, but he struggles on. His passionate pursuit has made a mess of his life, but his will to understand and to create is somehow awesome. Goethe has a choir of angels announce at the end of the play, "Whoever strives in ceaseless toil, him we may grant redemption." So, maybe this is how you cut a deal with the devil and still come out okay.

The Robert Johnson legend contains within it the lesson of craft integrity. It's the story of a man who changed his basic outlook on life, from one who first pursued happiness and pleasure directly – using his guitar and voice to get women and get local fame – to a man who pursued excellence instead, and then reaped rewards as a mere unintended consequence of that sacred pursuit. He didn't use music for personal gain. On the contrary, he sacrificed himself for the pursuit of musical excellence. But there's nothing about such pursuits that ensures recognition, or peer understanding, or celebrity status. That's why Johnson and all other Faustian characters are tragic. They are possessed by some sort of mysterious pursuit of excellence, and the personal consequences be damned.

Robert Johnson may have sold his soul, but he didn't sell out. There are many parallels between the extreme lives of Zen monks and blues artists, in this sense. Each has sacrificed the normal life of moderation and chosen to walk a desolate razor's edge. They are in their own ways extreme pathways, and as such they diverge from Gautama's original teachings of the Middle Way. But they provide wonderful icons of certain virtues, like dedication, endurance, and creativity – good work virtues. My own view is that these virtues can be practiced without giving up all the other aspects of a balanced life, but if you want to examine and reflect on such virtues, then the extreme cases are illuminating.

When I finally arrived in New Orleans, in search of my voodoo mojo, I binged on all the clichés. I ate embarrassing amounts of jambalaya and gumbo, watched a great street-band playing gospel favorites like "Just a Further Walk with Thee," indulged the Tarot card readers all along the cobbled streets, crammed in some sugar donuts and coffee at the Cafe du Monde, ogled some strippers that looked like rejects from a David Lynch film, and then passed out in a highly questionable hotel room. Hey, I said I was a Buddhist; I never said I was a first-rate Buddhist.

The next afternoon I found a good place to purchase my mojo bag. It was a voodoo shop off the beaten path and it was absolutely crammed with trinkets of weirdness. Like the "curiosity cabinets" of seventeenth-century Europe, this shop had a chaotic mixture of man-made and natural oddities bulging forth from every shelf – it was an over-stocked apothecary of magic totems. I found a bluish-purple satin draw-string bag about the size of a credit card. I began searching the store for voodoo objects of signifi-cance. The shelves had boxes of items and each box had a handscrawled sign that explained the specific powers of the item. For example, one box contained real alligator heads (each about the size of my hand), which seemed to have been sawed off their bodies and shellacked. I would have bought one but it wouldn't fit in my mojo bag. The sign on the alligator box said "Good for warding off evil in-laws." A sign on a box of tiny turtle shells said "Good for improving gambling luck."

I chose a little carved scarab beetle that seemed to be made of soap-stone in order to "Increase financial status." I also secured some very small seashells to "Ensure safe travel." But the real jewel in the crown was the swamp-rat's foot. It was the size and shape of my bent thumb and it was quite hideous, with sharp black claws and dark brown hair. The sign on the box assured me that this was the item to help with "Romantic Relations." At last, that infamous Muddy Waters charm would be mine! I didn't find any charms that improved musical ability per se, but I figured that the confluence of the other totems would suffice to help me be a better guitar player.

Well, I've had my mojo for a couple years now, and I can't tell if it's working. Maybe the problem is that I don't really believe in the power of a rat's foot, or a mojo even. Hell, not even Muddy Waters really believed it. He reveals in Robert Palmer's book *Deep Blues* that such voodoo stuff was popular among superstitious rural folk, but he didn't go in for supernaturalism. Buddhists all over Southeast Asia also love their superstitious amulets, and they make and trade elaborate talismans that are designed to give unearned skills and powers to the wearers. I've got a few of those, too.

My disbelief is bred partly from an overall dislike of superstition, which is, after all, one of the reasons I like philosophical Buddhism so much. But it also comes from a deep-seated distrust of all so-called quick fixes. You don't become excellent by carrying a mojo or an amulet, or by making a deal with the devil, or by sucking up to a corporate record executive, or by pretending to care about your craft (whatever it may be). Robert Johnson didn't become great because he drew up an unholy contract – and to think he did is to degrade the real *work* into which Johnson poured his heart. His real deal was to consecrate his life to music: to dedicate himself to practice, to the countless hours of skill-mastery, and to the amateur love of craft.

So, perhaps we have a response to my earlier question, Why is hard work, craft, and presence a better pathway than seeking celebrity status – especially when you can attain the benefits of being a star without the talent part? First, integrity in work or craft is how you own it – it's how you become the activity, or how you become an ingredient in the product you're making. Otherwise, you're just dancing with yourself outside the real action and pretending to be valuable. Second, becoming the activity is how you transcend your little ego – and that only happens when you're genuinely going for it, not when you're going through the motions. Finally, there is something inside you, that you carry around with you like a flame, when you have a hard-won set of skills. If you know how to build a sturdy chair, or play a fugue, or program code with precision, then you have something that can't be taken away from you. Nor does it need the external recognition of sycophants to give you fulfillment. External acknowledgment can come and go, but the internal happiness that comes from skillful action is intact either way.

In the *Dhammapada*, the Buddha describes the sad state of the impostor – the seeker of adulation and flattery. Even spiritual workers are susceptible to vanity, and Gautama cautions monks against the pursuit of celebrity. Such a fool "will wish for reputation, for precedence among the monks, for authority in the monasteries, and for veneration amongst the people. 'Let householders and hermits, both, think it was *I* who did that work; and let them ever ask me what they should do or not do.' These are the thoughts of the fool, puffed up with desire and pride. But one is the path of earthly wealth, and another is the path of *nirvana*. Let the follower of Buddha think of this and, without striving for reputation, let him ever strive after freedom" (V.71–75).

Chapter VII

Dharma and the Global Village

n addition to all the other reasons why I am a Buddhist, I have to add the final piece of the puzzle. As our world gets smaller and our many cultures, ideologies, and people start rubbing shoulders and bumping into each other more and more, Buddhism promises to be a polite, dignified, and tolerant contributor. Since it is not particularly interested in some invisible other world, it is more receptive to the needs of *this* world. The harm that intolerant ideological zealotry can do is manifest every day, but Buddhism is a philosophy of moderation – the Middle Way. It's so devoted to human liberation that it is willing to give *itself* up, if it is getting in the way of human flourishing. For example, the Buddha said that Buddhism is like a raft. Use the raft to navigate troubled waters, but when you've successfully reached the other shore, don't strap the cumbersome dinghy on your back to drag all over the land. I am a Buddhist because

Buddhism is tough enough to fight for social justice, but humble enough to get out of the way when it's not helping.

Today, Buddhism is a bigger player in the global political theater than any time in its past. We watch, for example, as Burmese monks get bloodied trying to protest against the military junta in Myanmar, we see riots and demonstrations erupting in Lhasa and ongoing bloodshed in Sri Lanka. In recent memory, we still have the Chinese Cultural Revolution and the Khmer Rouge's attempts to wipe out Buddhism in Cambodia. Buddhism's relevance in Asia has always been paramount, but the contemporary global village has rendered Buddhist politics more visible to Westerners. We in the West have taken a greater interest in parts of the world where Buddhists are under siege, and we've also become more interested in applying Buddhist ideas about conflict resolution to Western quarrels.

When Buddhism first spread in American popular culture, the Beats and hippies did not recognize much of a political dimension to Buddhism – indeed, its introverted apolitical quality was part of its attraction in those days. The nonviolent hippie Buddhism that most Americans are familiar with is an important part of Asian Buddhism. Nonviolence and the renunciation of aggression is a huge part of the original *dharma*. In fact, some twentieth-century Asian nationalists denounced the softer side of Buddhist culture and even blamed it for the successes of foreign imperialism. Chinese pragmatist philosopher Hu Shi (1891–1962) famously said, "Buddhism, which dominated Chinese religious life for twenty centuries, has reinforced the peaceful tendencies of an already too peaceful people." And when the Japanese nationalists, during the early Showa Period, wanted to strengthen their military aspirations, they did so in part by rejecting Buddhism and embracing a state-based Shinto religion.

Many Westerners are still scratching their heads about the various contemporary attacks on Buddhism and Buddhist practitioners. Why are governments regularly imprisoning and killing such peaceful, spiritual people? None of this will make sense unless we remind ourselves that there are three different forms of Buddhism: the *psychological* teachings (e.g., the Four Noble Truths and the abandonment of craving), the *philosophical* teachings (e.g., impermanence or *anicca*, and no-self or *anatta*, etc.), and the *cultural* traditions of Buddhism.

Cultural Buddhism

The cultural aspects of Buddhism are extremely diverse and have a very tenuous logical relation to its psychological and philosophical dimensions. It's no different in the West – one will search in vain, for example, to find Santa Claus and the Easter Bunny in the philosophical doctrines of Christianity, and yet they are significant aspects of Christian *cultures*. The same sort of cultural pastiche is found in Buddhist countries.

A few examples of cultural Buddhism will suffice to show the deviations between Gautama's teachings and the subsequent permutations. The most obvious is the fact that despite Gautama's constant refrain, that he was only a man and *not* to be worshipped, he was nonetheless deified in almost every subsequent culture of Buddhism. The Buddha insists that he is not a god, but as soon as he was dead, his followers started to characterize him as a god. So, the *devotional rituals* of Buddhism are very strong in Asia, and for most people, prayers and offerings to Buddhas and bodhisattvas, like Guan Yin, are even more important than the Four Noble Truths. In fact, it's fair to say that in China, Guan Yin, a derivative Buddhist "saint," is much more popular and prominent than Gautama and his teachings.

Another very telling example of cultural Buddhism can be found in one of the most popular stories in all of Asia, *Journey to the West (Xi you ji)*. Originally a Chinese folktale, based on the real Tang Dynasty monk Xuanzang (c. 602–664 CE), the story has found its way into all Chinese-influenced cultures, including Korean, Japanese, and Vietnamese. Xuanzang traveled to India (the West) to learn and copy the

Prajnaparamita scriptures – Mahayana sutras that were composed centuries after Gautama – and bring them back to the Chinese people. This much is factual. But Xuanzang's adventure along the silk route quickly became the stuff of legend and produced one of the most popular and powerful superheroes of Chinese culture, the monkey king, or Sun wu kong.

Sun wu kong is a petulant and mischievous monkey who studies Kung Fu and meditation and subsequently develops astounding superpowers that allow him to rival and harass the gods. He can make himself shrink to the size of a bug, or expand to the size of a city, or clone himself into an army of exact replicas, or fly on clouds, or bludgeon enemies with a magic cudgel, and so on. The Buddha tires of Sun wu kong's troublemaking, and eventually pins him under a mountain for thousands of years to teach him who's boss. Then comes the age of Xuanzang's journey to the West, and the Buddha frees Sun wu kong and gives him the job of serving as bodyguard for the Tang monk. What follows are wonderful adventures, in which the team of travelers (joined by two other flawed superheroes) fight evil and overcome temptation. It is a Buddhist story that is far more popular and well known in Asia than any of the Buddhist scriptures. And it does not portray Buddhism as a source of peacenik values and virtues. On the contrary, it gives us a Buddhism of *power*. It shows us a Buddhism that "takes names" and "kicks ass." It is the Buddhism of Kung Fu and martial arts generally. We'll return to this issue and follow up, but for now we'll sketch one more example of cultural Buddhism to help us clarify the political issues.

As I mentioned at the beginning of this book, one of the great advances of Buddhist *dharma* is its rejection of petrified social hierarchies. Recall how the Buddha criticized the Hindu caste system and also rejected the gender hierarchy by including women as travelers on the spiritual path. But this philosophical ideal, of a classless human race moving toward Buddha-hood, enjoyed a very short lifespan. In no time at all, female nunneries were closed down and women were forced back into more traditional social roles. In addition, some predictable changes occurred when the young upstart religion of Buddhism became the old entrenched and politically powerful ideology. As I mentioned before, it took a long time for Buddhism to gain ground in new territories, like China and Japan, but over centuries it became the preferred religion of some powerful leaders and emperors.

The once independent and apolitical monastic community became enmeshed in the affairs of state, and in some cases the highest-ranking religious leaders were also the most powerful sovereigns of the kingdom. The privileges once held by bloodline or caste designation or military might fell increasingly to the monastic communities. In some regions, monks became appendages of political power, and Buddhism became a cloak of respectability draped over the usual plundering of the ruling elite. This marriage between political power and Buddhism was not always bad, because the ideal Buddhist ruler – the *dhammaraja* – is a person who is supposed to rule with compassion and selfless strength. The Indian king Asoka (273–232 BCE), for example, is usually held up as a paragon of the virtuous Buddhist king, as is Jayavarman VII (1125–1215 CE) in Cambodia. Today many Thai people think of their king Bhumibol Adulyadej (1927–?) as a *dhammaraja*.

It is naive, however, to suppose that all powerful Buddhists were virtuous and altruistic. We cannot understand twentieth-century anti-Buddhist social revolutions, like those initiated by Mao Zedong and Pol Pot, until we understand that Buddhist monasteries were *perceived* (rightly or wrongly) as bastions of corruption and self-serving leadership. In Shanghai, for example, the Communists and Nationalists of the 1930s were outraged when they watched the head monk of Jing'an Temple prance around town with seven concubines – all of which had their own homes and cars. Such blatant disparity between wealthy monasteries and impoverished citizenry led to the often repeated revolutionary accusation that monks, like royalty, were "parasites" on the lifeblood of the workers.

Tibetan monasteries had become so corrupt that even the Thirteenth Dalai Lama, the reformer Thubten Gyatso (1876–1933), closed some monasteries and had monks flogged in the streets in an attempt to demote their power base. The entrenched Lhasa regime, made up of corrupt monks and wealthy families, had been heavily taxing the Tibetan lower classes for years. And in the early 1950s both the Panchen Lama and the Fourteenth Dalai Lama actually welcomed Mao's "liberation" of Tibet.

During the Great Leap Forward (1958–1961) and the Cultural Revolution (1966–1976), Maoists engaged in a strident "leveling" program. Tibet and the entire mainland of China were turned upside down in an attempt to redistribute the wealth and property – pulling it out of the hands of corrupt monasteries (and the bourgeoisie generally) and spreading it among the workers. At least that was the ideal goal.

The excesses of the social revolutions are well known. Many good people were persecuted and died because they were painted with the broad brush of "corruption" or "parasitic class" or whatever. My own father-in-law, a professor from Nanjing China, was sent to a "reeducation camp" for many years, for no other reason except that he was a learned scholar. So, let it be known that I am not a fan of the revolution per se. But it is also important to understand the legitimate impulse to root out corruption and unjust hierarchy as it existed in Buddhist countries. In some places, Buddhist monks were living like princes and the laypersons were living like dogs.

So, here is yet another example of the way that Buddhist *culture* can evolve differently from the other strands of Buddhist *philosophy* and *psychology*. The original *dharma* tries to eliminate unjust social hierarchies, but throughout history Buddhism has found itself (just like every other religion) caught up in the many reversals of the haves-and have-nots. Drawing these distinctions between philosophy, psychology, and culture helps us to make sense of some of the political violence that Buddhism has encountered in the past century. There appear to be four basic kinds of attacks on contemporary Buddhism – attacks that will probably continue into the future.

The Four Big Attacks on Buddhism

First is the criticism I've just sketched. Some Buddhist monasteries became powerful and corrupt, and social reformers tried to break that hegemony by violent means. In this opposition, there is no particular censure or attack on Buddhism per se, but only an assault on corruption – corruption that happened to be dressed up in monks' robes. Second, we find Buddhism ensnared in ongoing nationalist battles. Besides being a spiritual path, Buddhism is a major source of national and ethnic identity in places like Cambodia, Thailand, Sri Lanka, Tibet, and so on. We in the States live in such a comparatively pluralistic melting pot that we forget how religion can be integral to turf wars. Tamil Tigers in Sri Lanka, for example, frequently targeted Buddhist monks and monasteries – even massacring a bus full of young monks in 1987, because the majority population is Buddhist and the minority Tamils want to break away as a separate country. Or consider the ongoing violence in southern Thailand, where Buddhist monks and laypeople are regularly killed by Muslim separatists. In these cases, Buddhism is being targeted because it happens to be the state religion of those governments that are under siege. Terrorists are seeking to provoke the majority governments in those regions.

A third reason for violence against Buddhism is particularly tragic. When Buddhist monks are being good Buddhists (i.e., not corrupt), then they frequently act as the conscience of a country. Living outside the realm of power politics and earthly pursuits, Buddhist monks frequently agitate for the oppressed and exploited members of society – they speak truth to power. "Engaged Buddhism" is the name that's often given to the pursuit of social justice. Many monastic communities have put themselves on the frontlines of antigovernment protests, and corrupt governments have responded by pummeling them. Buddhist monks have a long tradition of protesting corruption in their own countries, and this has brought terrible violence upon them. Vietnamese, Cambodian, Burmese, Tibetan, Laotian, and Chinese monks, among others, have all been targeted at one time or another by their own governments. Because they are not interested in *desire* or *profit* or *fame*, Buddhists are perfectly positioned to play the role of "justice gadflies" in their own country. Like all martyrs for justice, they pay a very high price.

The fourth kind of attack on Buddhism is the only *philosophical* one. It's the one that criticizes the ideas of the *dharma* per se. As such, the confrontation is relatively bloodless. It's the claim, which I mentioned earlier, that Buddhism is too peaceful, too acquiescent, too detached from politics. The criticism is often trotted out by Easterners who want to prevent foreign rule or foreign bullying, and more recently some Western scholars have been using it to "explain" the susceptibility of Asians to fascist political regimes. Like Malcolm X's claim that "Christianity failed black people" because it led them to focus on the *next* life instead of *this* unjust one, so, too, critics of Buddhism have claimed that the doctrine of "all things must pass" has only succeeded in resigning Asian people to unhappy material conditions. What is needed, these critics suggest, is more active fighting for justice, not quiet detachment. The idea that acquiescence to autocrats is "more prevalent" in Asia than the West is so patently absurd, and disproved by a glance at history, that I'm not even going to address it. But the overall critique – Buddhism is too peaceful – is worth examining.

Power Buddhism

Is Buddhism a "weakling" – a sunken-chested coward, getting sand kicked in its face by buff bullies? He-man writer Robert Louis Stevenson despised Henry David Thoreau's detached philosophy, and one can imagine a similar objection to Buddhism. Stevenson said, "Thoreau's content and ecstasy in living was, we may say, like a plant that he had watered and tended with womanish solicitude; for there is apt to be something unmanly, something almost dastardly, in a life that does not move with dash and freedom, and that fears the bracing contact of the world. In one word, Thoreau was a skulker. He did not wish virtue to go out of him among his fellow-men, but slunk into a corner to hoard it for himself. He left all for the sake of certain virtuous self-indulgences." Many people have imagined Buddhism in similar terms.

I find this kind of objection to Buddhism unconvincing for several reasons. While it is true that Buddhism has a strong peacenik tendency in the *dharma* – reduction of inner and outer conflict – it also has an astoundingly *popular* tendency, albeit lesserknown in the West, of "power Buddhism." The idea that Buddhism and Buddhists are "weak" is entirely the product of a certain kind of inaccurate marketing. If you live in Asian cultures for a while, you will find people conceptualizing and enacting a tougher, stronger Buddhism. The Buddha and the *dharma* also represent sources of strength. Power is necessary, because life is struggle. Even the ultimate goal of detached equanimity can only come after substantial struggle.

The Chinese story of *Journey to the West (Xi you ji)*, which I mentioned earlier, is a wonderful example of this more masculine Buddhism. Contrary to the hippie Western version of Buddhism, which took its shape as a critique of American war, the righteous and virtuous characters of *Xi you ji* regularly employ force and coercion to bring miscreants under the rule of Buddhism. The Tang monk Xuan Zang, for example, uses a magical headband to compel the monkey king to submit to his rule. The headband, given to Xuan Zang by Guan Yin, is irremovably fastened to the monkey king's head, and when the monk chants the sutras the headband tightens and forces him to his knees in pain. This Buddhist-sanctioned force goes on repeatedly throughout the story – but we see that Sun wu kong *needs* this kind of discipline to be a better being. The Buddha himself tricks

Sun wu kong and overpowers him by magically expanding his hand to the size of the universe to capture the wily and disrespectful monkey in his grip. And the many enemies of the monk and his Buddhist quest are vanquished with moral force and violence. Numerous stories of struggle, failure, struggle, submission, and mastery make up the narrative of *Journey to the West*. We repeatedly find a muscular Buddhism that we can rely upon to help us in the trials and tribulations of our beleaguered lives.

But we don't have to go back centuries to find this tough Buddhism incarnate, and we don't have to go to literature to find it. The most visible political issue connected to Buddhism, in our own day, is surely the China–Tibet tension. This story is so complex that it requires another book to analyze it, so I can't say much in this context. But a couple of insights are relevant to the question of "power Buddhism." As it is currently framed by Western media, the morality play is between the peaceful and mystical Tibetans (symbolized by the Dalai Lama) and the aggressive secular Chinese. The Free Tibet movement has simplified matters and made assumptions about both sides that do not bear out under scrutiny. Perhaps the most misunderstood issue is that, contrary to most Western perceptions, the current Dalai Lama has never advocated independence for Tibet. From the late 1950s to the present, he has always disagreed with the

Tibetan nationalist rebels, and he has praised the important modernization that China has brought to Tibet. What he wants is a Middle Way that balances Chinese progress with a greater Tibetan political voice. But this is only a political point and I mention it to demonstrate the extent of Western misperceptions. The more salient point, for our discussion of "power Buddhism," is the reality of Tibetan Buddhism itself.

The current Dalai Lama, Tenzin Gyatso, is indeed a paragon of peaceful serenity, but he is not representative of the long history of muscular Buddhism that has dominated Tibet – a history conveniently unknown in the West. Previous Dalai Lamas have been extremely belligerent. The Lama before Tenzin Gyatso was actually known as the "Bodhisattva Warrior." He was a powerful political and military fighter, who raised an army and fiercely fought the British, the Chinese, and his own people. Historian Lee Feigon, in his *Demystifying Tibet*, tells an anecdote of how *earthly* the Bodhisattva Warrior could be. When the Lama suspected that an enemy had tried to put a hex on him, by sewing a voodoo-doll into his shoes, the outraged Lama ordered the offender to be "immersed in a huge copper vat until he drowned." And such violence was not isolated, but a regular part of Tibetan politics.

After the Bodhisattva Warrior died, and before the current Lama was chosen, there was a struggle for power in the 1930s. When a reformer named Tsepon Lungshor tried to undermine the abusive Lhasa monasteries, he was accused of "Bolshevism" and the head monks sentenced him to be blinded by having his eyes pulled out. They twisted a tourniquet on his temples until the pressure forced one eyeball to pop out, but when the other wouldn't pop, they cut it out and cauterized everything with boiling oil. So much for the image of Tibet and Tibetan Buddhism as an eternal archetype of peace.

I offer these examples of Buddhist culture, not as a condemnation of Buddhism, but as a way to address the gulf between the perception and the reality of Buddhism. Buddhism is not a wilting flower of passive submission. Those critics, East and West, who imagine it as an emasculating cultural force, have not studied much Buddhist history. To the above examples, we can add the huge culture of Shaolin Buddhist Kung Fu, Japanese Zen martial arts, monkled social protests, and unflinching monk self-immolations.

I finish this point about "power Buddhism" with a positive and illuminating allegory from Cambodian monk Maha Ghosananda. When I was living in Cambodia, I had the good fortune to meet the very powerful Maha Ghosananda before he died. He demonstrated the strength of Buddhism by defying the anti-Buddhist Khmer Rouge in the 1970s and by leading many peace marches in the face of terrible threats and even attacks. He tells a story about the need to balance compassion with wisdom. One must strive for tolerance, openness, and compassionate acceptance, but one shouldn't be naive about it. Maha Ghosananda's parable tells of a violent dragon who met a bodhisattva on the road one day. The bodhisattva told the dragon that he should not kill anymore and should instead adopt the Buddhist precepts and care for all life. The bodhisattva inspired the dragon, and afterward the dragon became completely nonviolent. But now the children who tended to the animal flocks nearby, seeing that the dragon had become gentle, lost all fear of him. And they began to torment him, stuffing stones and dirt into his mouth, pulling on his tail, and jumping on his head.

Soon the dragon stopped eating and became very sick. When the dragon encountered the bodhisattva again, he complained, "You told me that if I kept the precepts and was compassionate, I would be happy. But now I suffer, and I am not happy at all." To this the bodhisattva replied, "My son, if you have compassion, morality, and virtue, you must also have wisdom and intelligence. This is the way to protect yourself. The next time the children make you suffer, show them your fire. After that, they will trouble you no more."

The Fifth Attack: Missionary Opportunists in War-Torn Lands

Another aspect of globalization, besides the political, which impacts Buddhism directly is the ongoing struggle between *religious* ideologies. When I lived in Cambodia, for example, many Christian missionaries had recently come to the country to try to win it over for Christ. Cambodia, like other war-torn developing countries, had lost a generation to violence and with that human loss also came a cultural loss. Buddhism had been targeted as "outmoded tradition" by the Khmer Rouge and it was almost completely stamped out. This left a huge ideological hole in the Cambodian psyche. Aggressive Protestant evangelists from the West explicitly target such vulnerable communities and descend, as soon as it's safe, to convert the "heathen." In developing countries, they go to poor communities and offer the starving locals a bag of rice if they come to church and get baptized as Christians. These rice briberies are common in Southeast Asia, and demonstrate the state of religious warfare in a globalized world. Granted, this kind of warfare is much better than the old bloody versions, but it's still repugnant.

Perhaps my earlier list of four criticisms of Buddhism should be increased to include this fifth attack. Christians who want to supplant Buddha with Jesus are convinced that Buddhism is simply false, whereas Christianity is true. The missionaries I met in Cambodia were confident that Jesus was God incarnate, whereas Buddha was just a man – and why would anybody prefer a man, no matter how smart, to God himself? Buddhists, according to these evangelists, need to get on the winning team.

It remains to be seen how these religious competitions will play out. Religions meet each other like tectonic plates. They can press against each other interminably, building up a mountain of strain – with neither side giving an inch, or the meeting can become a subduction zone where one tradition folds under the other and slowly melts away. A place where such seismic shifts will be happening on a very great scale is certainly China.

In 2005 President George W. Bush visited China to meet with President Hu Jintao. While there, he provocatively attended services at one of the only state-sanctioned Protestant churches in Beijing. During his visit, Bush encouraged China to expand its religious freedoms and President Hu was ostensibly receptive to the issue. Bush repeated the visit to a church and the entreaty when he attended the 2008 Beijing Olympics. In April 2006, China hosted the World Buddhist Forum – China's first international religious meeting since the Communists swept to power more than five decades ago. Organizers timed the forum to coincide with the Christian festival of Easter, apparently to send a message of China's greater religious tolerance to Western watchers.

China has had a dubious relationship with its religious minorities for the past century – most recently, the Falun Gong movement has been targeted by the Chinese government (a crackdown in 1999 and highly disputed case of self-immolation at Tiananmen Square in 2001 have led the international community to take notice and even characterize the issue as a human rights question).

In the 1920s there were several anti-Christian movements in China, and after the civil war and the rise of Mao's PRC (People's Republic of China), all forms of religion became relegated to underground cultural expressions at best. Mao and the Communist Party of China saw religion, whether it be Tibetan Buddhism, Chinese Confucianism, or Christianity, as "unscientific," "hierarchical," and "corrupting." Mao agreed with Marx's famous view of religion as the "opiate of the masses."

Today, as China opens up, Christianity struggles for official recognition but thrives under the radar as small localized "house churches."

The government puts the figure at 20 million Christians in China today (still a small number when one remembers that China has 1.3 billion people – over four times the United States), but nongovernmental groups (NGOs) estimate the number much higher (and David Aikman, author of *Jesus in*

Beijing, puts the figure closer to 85 million). Buddhism is back on the rise again in China too, but not with the gusto and panache of Christianity.

As a Buddhist, I'm obviously rooting for Buddhism in the coming competition for Chinese spiritual ideology. I hope China does *not* become a Christian nation. I say this not because I have something against Christianity (a deep and beautiful religion), but because I have great respect for the ancient spiritual and philosophical traditions of the Far East (Confucianism, Daoism, and Buddhism). If I were a devout Christian I should no doubt be happy that the gospel is on the rise in China and the "pagan" beliefs may get trampled under righteous foot. But I'm not happy.

China's Tsunamis of Change and Their Impact on Buddhist Traditions

Much is written these days about the economic explosion in China, but little ink is spilled about the deep cultural changes currently going on in China. While the Western media focuses on stories about increasing international economic influence and occasional human rights abuses (the latter story growing quieter as the former story grows louder), we in the West are largely unaware of the intellectual and spiritual sea-changes taking shape inside China.

When Mao famously swept the country clean of ancient indigenous ideologies (read Confucianism and Buddhism), he created a generation (or two) of "blank slates." Of course, no one is ever really a blank slate – ancient cultural tendencies go underground when propagandists start their sweeping. But the effect of the communist repression of religion upon the family was a generational reticence to explicitly transmit religious teachings. Why would I, the parental logic goes, transmit dangerous ideas to my child? Maybe I, as parent, believe in Buddhism or maybe I don't care much one way or the other, but I certainly want to protect my child from whatever miseries I can (e.g., reeducation camps or worse). The result of this logic is that people who educated their children (from the 1960s down to the present) did so by skipping the classics or humanities and stressing instead the useful skills of modernity (e.g., engineering, science, city planning, accounting, etc.). Avoiding the humanities, including Buddhism, was a smart strategy for parents who wanted the best for their kids. But now it is time to reap what was sown.

As China leaps ahead, its young population (the wealthiest demographic) knows very little about its own literature, arts, philosophy, and religion. Of course, some people run in the rat race all their lives and never develop a taste for questions like "what does it all mean?" but most people eventually ponder the bigger mysteries of their existence. In previous ages, one would, if gripped by a philosophical mood, simply turn to the great indigenous works of Chinese intellectual culture: Kongzi's (Confucius's) *Analects*, Laozi's *Daodejing*, the Buddha's *Sutras*, and so forth. But these days such fountains of wisdom are like trickling rivulets in the landscape of religious competition, and the Christian Bible is often more readily available to the average spiritual searcher.

In December 2006, a group of PhD students from China's top universities circulated an online plea to "wake up the Chinese people to resist the Western cultural invasion" – in particular, to discourage the Chinese fascination with Christmas. The *China Daily* (December 28, 2006) predicted that the petition would likely be drowned out by Chinese Christmas revelers; after all, "Christmas and Valentine's Day are becoming more popular than the Spring Festival among youngsters."

Much of this recent fascination with Christianity is purely fashionable – I can't tell you how many times I heard Christmas songs ring-tones on kids' cell-phones when I lived in Shanghai. Christianity is attractive to Chinese because it's exotic and obviously associated with successful Western modernity. But some of the fascination runs much deeper. Over 40 million Chinese-language Bibles are floating around the mainland now, with more on the way – many young people are reading the Good Book and taking it to heart. What are the deeper reasons for Christianity's popularity among younger Chinese?

I suspect that one of the reasons why Christianity might be more enticing to young Chinese has to do with the fact that traditional Chinese culture believes in public morality. From Confucius up through Mao's communism, the Chinese character is shaped by shame and honor – both public, observable, social relations. Subsequently, Chinese kids are raised in a pressure cooker of public scrutiny – a severe meritocracy, wherein your grades are put on public display for all to see, your rank in the *danwei* (work unit) is known to all, and your every career and personal decision reflects on your family's good name – and on your ancestors too. In short, your worth and value is defined in large part by the community.

Christianity offers a very tempting reprieve from all this public morality. In a strict meritocracy, like China's, there's lots of public praise and celebration for those few who excel at the top – but a whole lot more shame and disgrace for the majority of people who failed to make the top notch. Christianity comes to China with a hero, Jesus, who appeared to everybody like a failure – Romans, Jews, even his disciples, were pretty sure, as he struggled on the cross, that he was a loser. But, contrary to all public appraisal of his worth, Jesus was somebody. And not just somebody, but the "greatest."

Here, then is a very consoling message to a people who feel that they've been misjudged and misunderstood by the public culture. Christianity comes to average Chinese persons, and assures them that they are somebody. They can have a personal, internal, relationship with themselves (and God), and no amount of public judgment can take that worth and value away from them.

While I understand this attraction to Christianity, my own hope is that China will turn back to its own traditions rather than simply adopting Christianity. Confucian and then communist cultures, with their public, shame-based moralities, have indeed put a great stress on Chinese people, but their own lost Buddhism is a wonderful source of private worth and integrity. China should be rescuing its own Buddhism, which was lost during the revolution – but it should be bringing back a purer version of the *dharma*, stripped of the lazy devotional and superstitious aspects and of the corrupt social hierarchies of the old days.

Where Will Buddhism Land in Our Clash of Civilizations?

My reasons for preferring and recommending Buddhism over Christianity should not surprise you at this stage in the book. I think the Buddha's teachings about freeing the mind from suffering are empirically testable and do not require commitments to mystical, supernatural metaphysics. Christianity, like Islam, Judaism, Hinduism, and animism, requires many metaphysical commitments – none of which seem testable or even reasonable. The reason why I think less metaphysics is preferable to more metaphysics is that unverifiable beliefs about ultimate reality are always great sources of prejudice and bigotry. But more important, supernatural beliefs do little or nothing to remove the human suffering caused by craving – in fact, such beliefs only seem to add to it. In an increasingly globalized world, where a major feature of that globalization is the spread of consumerism, it would be a shame to see such a powerful antidote to consumerism, Buddhism, slip away in the competition of religions. But the juggernaut of consumerism may eventually ensure a global religion that distracts people with superstition and keeps them craving and buying.

I also don't know how Buddhism will play out in the larger so-called clash of civilizations between Islamic fundamentalism and Western ideologies. It seems clear that Americans will be in some sort of "war on terror" for many years to come, perhaps indefinitely. The threat of real enemies has brought out the best and the worst in Americans: profound compassion and shocking vengeance. Both these emotional "animals" live inside each American. Most of us are first pulled toward tribal feelings of me-and-mine, and then pulled toward egalitarian feelings of fairness for all, and then pulled back again. Both impulses, tribalism and egalitarianism, are vying for control in politics and in human psychology. Who knows how this will all play out?

Tribal-based cultures, like Arab culture, for example, are also honor based cultures. For all their faults they are fiercely protective of family and clan. Buddhism, like Christianity, pushes us away from the natural biases of human nature – it pushes us beyond the usual concentric circles of value that surround our own families and seeks to expand the circle to include all people, all animals, all beings. The West has been pursuing this same model, in secular form, for several centuries now. We can trace the development from Luther's Reformation up through Enlightenment Kantian morality that asked us to treat *all* people equally as "ends in themselves" rather than "means" to some end. And after Immanuel Kant, we have the utilitarian tradition that asked us to maximize the greatest happiness for the greatest number of people, and finally the "fairness" philosophy of John Rawls and the rejection of personal bias, nepotism, favoritism, preferential treatment, and partiality. Discordant on almost every other point of comparison, Buddhism, Christianity, and Western liberalism all make strange bedfellows on this one point of egalitarianism.

While such impartiality is often championed in the West as a sign of civilization and superiority, I suspect we've been insincere – even with ourselves. I never felt the tribal impulse so strong in myself, for example, than when I became a parent. Not only am I *biased* in favor of my son, but I'll chop your fucking head off if you put him in danger. Okay ... see what I mean?

We often compare the impulses of tribalism and egalitarianism and tell ourselves and everybody else, loudly, that the equality value system is the "correct"one and the biased value system is "incorrect"or certainly primitive. I can't really accept this easy formula, and suspect that our value conflicts are more complicated. For example, not only does parenting or family change the weighting distribution of human value, but even friendship flies in the face of egalitarianism. My friend is more important than a mere acquaintance or a total stranger. They are not equal, and my friend is not going to be my friend for long if I regularly slight his happiness in favor of the majority's. Nor am I going to feel the special experiences of friendship, which is inherently preferential, if my friend regularly rebuffs my requests with the moral high-ground of principled fairness to all.

I mention all this to place Buddhism in a context of competing global ideologies, but also to acknowledge that Buddhism competes with the human heart itself. Many piously detached proponents of Buddhism will simply avoid the tension by giving up on their inner tribalism – denying it, repressing it, shunning it, or taking a sadomasochistic approach to it. Not me.

On the other side, many resolutely attached people will smell the insincerity in the overly righteous Buddhism, and gladly kick it to the curb in favor of their strong kinship ties. I feel the wisdom in both sides. Even the Buddha, for example, had a best friend, named Ananda. One can only assume that some sort of special or elevated value bonded Gautama and Ananda to each other. It is preference and bias and partiality, after all, that makes your best friend a best friend. And there is no need for apology in this. I can't help but think that Buddhism – with its stress on the Middle Way – can either find a future integration of tribalism and egali-tarianism, or at least help us to better live with an irresolvable, irreconcilable tension in the human heart.

The Music

In the beginning of this book I compared practicing Buddhism to the difficult journey of learning to play a musical instrument. If, as I've just suggested, there really is an irreconcilable tension in the human heart, then we might learn to accept it in the same way we accept tension in music.

Bach, the Beatles, and Kurt Cobain would all be dry as dust if they didn't twist some dissonance into their music, if only to make the tonal resolutions powerful. I think the melody of Buddhism weaves between the sickly sweet major scale and the sour dissonance of the diminished or tri-tone scales. It plays somewhere between the Pollyanna warm-and-fuzzy tones and the gloomy nihilistic ones.

I've been a Buddhist for twenty years and a musician for twenty-five. The analogy is quite strong. In both ventures, my skills wane significantly if I don't practice. And even when my "chops" are strong, a slight turn can reveal whole traditions and genres that utterly humble me. Sometimes I challenge myself and run headlong at stuff that's over my head, and other times I lay back and just find the groove. My goal is not extreme virtuosity in Buddhism or music, but well-rounded living. I'd like to spend forty more years exploring the many tonal variations, harmonies, and rhythms of Buddhism. Maybe if I make it to 80 years old, I'll write a much more melodic book about "Why I *was* a Buddhist" but until then, I'll just try to stay in tune.